Attach Me If You Can

Attach Me If You Can

*"How to help children attach,
feel safe and ultimately act lovable."*
Phillip D. Hamberg, L.M.S.W., L.M.F.T.

PUBLISHING

Belleville, Ontario, Canada

ATTACH ME IF YOU CAN

Copyright © 2011, Phillip Hamberg

ISBN: 978-1-55452-736-6
LSI Edition: 978-1-55452-737-3
E-book ISBN: 978-1-55452-738-0

Cover design by Ellen Allderink

Cataloguing data available from Library and Archives Canada

To order additional copies, visit:
www.essencebookstore.com

For more information, please contact:
Phillip D. Hamberg
Email: phamberg@att.net
Phone: 616-669-1717

Essence Publishing

20 Hanna Court, Belleville, Ontario, Canada K8P 5J2.
Phone: 1-800-238-6376. Fax: (613) 962-3055.
Email: info@essence-publishing.com
Web site: www.essence-publishing.com

Printed in Canada
by

Essence
PUBLISHING

Contents

Introduction

The capacity to relate, to love, to feel without fear, to impart hope, and to critically interpret in an acceptable manner are gifts that were given to me through decades of faithful partnering with others, in particular through the unfailing love of my precious wife, Patricia, whom I have been privileged to be married to for forty years.

After more than thirty years of treating children and adults in psychotherapy and countless hours giving workshops on everything from attachment disorders and emotional trauma to boundary conflicts and behavior problems among staff, I have been encouraged by others to put my thoughts into writing. I make no claim to genius status or having extra sensory insight; I confess that what I know my clients have taught me, sometimes painstakingly and always patiently. For that I am in their debt. I am not a star but only a man reflecting the light and wisdom of countless others.

I must begin with a disclaimer.

This book makes no claims of scientific authenticity, in-depth research, or profound psychological discoveries. It has no review of literature; nor does it have an extensive bibliography. This book is about what I personally have found to be helpful in my work with children and adults; however, the main focus will be the child.

My hope is that the reader will build on what I have integrated and learned and will find this book practical for everyday work.

I have organized this book as I would do a lecture series: in an informal, conversational style. Each chapter could essentially stand alone and be referenced by itself; however, if the book is taken as a whole the reader will comprehend a more integrated sense of the developing person. There is no one solid theory base that I espouse to, but the serious reader will quickly ascertain my bias for attachment theory and object relations theory, with just enough psychoanalytic theory and ego psychology to keep the quickly bored from nodding off (I hope).

If you read this book with an eye toward working with children, I believe a large number of usable corrective measures will leap out at you that can be helpful.

In the first half of the book, entitled "The Way It's Supposed to Be," I cover good mental health, starting with early development and individuation (Margaret Mahler). I then continue into how this "good enough" (Donald Winnicott) development flows into academic performance and how the young school student views the world. The second half of the book, entitled "The Way It Is," is initially a tad more depressing but potentially very helpful. I will deal with nurturing gone awry and issues like unintentional emotional neglect, but be assured that corrective measures will be included at every point.

If you work with children, have children, or remember being a child, I hope you find this book stimulating, thought provoking, and, above all, helpful.

Part 1

The Way It's Supposed to Be

CHAPTER 1

What Is Good Mental Health?

The Internet includes at least 400,000 different Web sites defining good mental health, listing hundreds of attributes and behaviors. There are many more Web sites that define good mental health as an absence of pathological symptoms and then list those symptoms ad nauseam. I prefer to describe good mental health in positive terms, with a list of proactive things that one can do to maintain or achieve good mental health. Being ever the reductionist, I like to describe good mental health in general terms by using ten proactive talking points.

The first attribute of good mental health is a realistic and accurate view of one's self and others. Infants as young as ten days old attempt to obtain an accurate view of themselves by how other people treat them. Babies and young children take their cues from others and respond positively to being smiled at, talked to, and generally positively acknowledged. They respond to things like people enjoying being around them, people touching them in a loving and appropriate manner, and people responding to and reading their cues when they need something.

It's fascinating to watch babies as they watch the environment and the people within it. Babies actually "listen" with their eyes and are exquisitely perceptive as to people's intent because of visual cues. Masad Khan writes in the journal the *Psychoanalytic Study of the Child* that babies can figure out whether or not they are safe within their environment within ten days after being born.[1] How they are treated gives them a view of self and also gives a "projected" view of others based on how the child is treated.

If a baby is treated harshly or roughly, the baby starts to feel as if he or she deserves to be treated poorly because he or she is not a good person. The child also projects those feelings onto other people and expects other people to be not good, loving, or nurturing in return. It is difficult for a young child or baby to have a view of self that isn't based upon how others treat him or her. This is why it is so essential that babies and young children are touched warmly, talked with appropriately, and responded to quickly when their needs arise.

As they grow and realize that they are separate from their caregivers, children start to understand that not everyone will always embrace their brilliance or their needs. As children mature past the preschool age and have to live in their own bodies, having an accurate view of self becomes more important. If the young child's nurturing needs have not been met with appropriate responses, the child tends to grow up being much more concerned about what others do and get.

We see many children in elementary school who are so concerned about what others get and what they might be missing that it is difficult for them to know who they are and what their own specific needs are. These children become very "other" oriented in the sense that they tend to want to live almost in other people's bodies, which tells you a little about the lack of satisfaction that they feel living in their own.

An elementary age child who does not live in his or her own body but is constantly needing others to give direction, tell him or her what to do, and reassure him or her every step of the way is like a child who is drowning and sees someone else's life flash before his or her eyes. This is a child who cannot self-regulate. It's interesting to note also the stress levels in these children, as indicated by nervous habits, frequent crying, or fits of temper or rage. These children tend to be difficult to soothe and, when they receive soothing, are generally unable to trust it as genuine.

A realistic and accurate view of one's self basically means "Does the person truly know that he or she is lovable?" Knowing that one is lovable opens up numerous doors for a feeling of safety, being attached, and belonging.

The second characteristic of good mental health is an accurate perception of the environment. The environment of a five-month-old is significantly smaller than the environment of a five-year-old. A five-month-old child is environmentally bound to "significant love objects," such as the mother, father, grandparents, and siblings. The five-year-old, on the other hand, may have preschool teachers, a peer group, and other social networks. How we perceive our environment is, again, based on the kind of treatment that we have received, and, barring genetic anomalies and people who actually hurt us, our perception of the environment should be one of positive anticipation and a sense of trust.

While it is inaccurate to view all of the environment as a trusting environment, especially in the world that we live in today, the trick is to help children develop an accurate perception of their environment as being both good and bad and an understanding that people have unique combinations of both good and bad traits. The vast majority of people are not out to purposely make another's life miserable; however, there are times when people certainly are miserable and do go out of their way to make things uncomfortable.

The accurate perception of people as a combination of both good and bad is essential for young children to develop in order to maintain a consistent relationship with any one person. Children will find that even their beloved mother at times is scary when she screams or gets angry. However, a child who is "held" in Mother's mind as valuable and consistently important will understand that even mommy is a curious combination of actions that may sometimes be scary and other times wonderful. (We will talk about this later under the topic "The Capacity to Tolerate Ambivalence.")

Children also learn through having an accurate perception of the environment that the vast majority of people are not going to meet every need that they have. Children are born and develop narcissistically, or egocentrically, which means they consider the self to be the center of the universe. This perception is a struggle within the child as early as eighteen months of life, but by the age of three children should have an accurate view that they in fact are not the center of the universe. The child is subject to immediate regression in the face of trauma or extreme need.

People who develop past the age of three and hang on to a great deal of egocentrism expect others to meet their needs and expect them to know what they want even before they speak. Some of my adult clients, usually female, will complain about dating a man who is egocentric and requires that she surround him with love and affection and meet his every whim. To hang on to a view that is egocentric past the age of five will not serve the developing person well and certainly will not promote good relationships and human interaction.

If in fact the child lives within an abusive or neglectful environment, the accurate perception of that environment may be very negative. The danger here lies in the child expecting that all environments will be like the one he or she lives in. The child in turn projects negativity onto other people and even at times attempts to elicit negative behavior as a method of creating an environment he or she understands.

The third characteristic of good mental health is the willingness to accept one's own strengths and weaknesses. Young children need adults to help them to recognize their strengths. Children usually identify their own strengths as things they enjoy. They also identify their strengths when people show appreciation for the tasks that they do. One boy said to me, "When I do things good, people thank me." Conversely, the weaknesses usually are identified as "things I hate to do" or things they do but feel they do inadequately. Again, in this case children "hear" approval or disapproval in other people's faces.

Children who have been hurt and who do not trust other people will deny that they have any strengths, sometimes openly but many times unconsciously. It is not unusual for a child to be appreciated or be told that he or she has a specific strength and then completely deny that anyone has mentioned this to him or her. In fact, when you ask such children what their strengths are, they simply cannot recall.

For teachers dealing with such children, I often recommend a P.E. (positive experience) book. Children who have poor self-esteem and who cannot accept their own strengths or see them often find it helpful for the teacher to record these strengths in a spiral notebook and allow the child to refer back to the pages that note his or her accomplishments. The entries are signed and dated by the teacher. Teachers have told me that if they allow students to take the books home to show their parents, the books inevitably get lost, indicating again an unconscious denial that they are capable of having strengths or positive characteristics. Children need to know that they are curious combinations of strong points and weak points as well as good actions and bad actions. To accept oneself as a "whole" person (having both good and bad traits) is extremely helpful for the mental health of the developing child.

The fourth characteristic of good mental health is the ability to live in the present but have long-range goals. This is a cognitive capacity that really is not set in place until the child is at least three years old and has the ability to represent pictures mentally. When the child starts living attentively and has pictures of where he or she might be one month, two months, three months from now, we know that the child is developing the capacity for good mental representation and projecting out into the future, which represents hope. It is essential that the developing person have hope that he or she will grow, achieve, and be interacted with on a positive level.

I cannot tell you how many children I have seen who have little to no ability to see themselves in the future doing anything and, in fact, have no hope that anything positive will happen to them tomorrow, let alone next month. These children are often unable to answer the question "What do you want to be when you grow up?" To assess children who are struggling emotionally, this is one of the telltale questions I can ask in terms of how they view themselves in the future.

Good mental health, therefore, is three dimensional in the sense that a child needs a positive nurturing past, a nurturing and reciprocal interaction in the present, and a mental representation (picture) that his or her actions and interactions will produce positive results in the future.

A fifth characteristic of good mental health is possessing a system of values, including clear standards of what is right and what is wrong. A value system and a conscience simply do not develop by themselves, and we are not genetically endowed with them.

One four-year-old defined conscience as "when you hear your mommy's voice on the inside." Selma Fraiberg, author of The Magic Years, states that children are "little savages" who need to be socialized. Socialization comes in the context of caring, nurturing, reciprocal interaction.

When a child starts caring about someone else, I assume that the child has a "significant love object" on the inside of himself or herself. I have found, however, that it is possible to be a caring person without that love object represented on the inside. Children who are left to nurture themselves sometimes do so by nurturing others in a kind of vicarious nurturing process. Children who know the "right thing to do" even when no one is watching are children who have mentors, loved ones, and significant love objects firmly planted on the inside, and they carry those voices in their minds.

Nothing is more terrifying to me as a therapist than to see a child with little or no conscience. These children are capable of doing any kind of hurt to another person and suffer no pains of guilt or remorse. I heartily endorse a "healthy" amount of guilt within each child. Like a conscience, guilt is only produced in the context of a nurturing attachment.

When children do not have a clear system of right and wrong, they tend to be narcissistic and self-centered, acting solely in accordance with their own needs. The self-serving child is easily bored and in need of constant stimulation. This stimulation need is often expressed in inappropriate, overly aggressive, and sometimes violent behavior. This kind of child just seems to be looking for trouble.

The sixth characteristic of good mental health is having a sense of independence and autonomy while at the same time realizing and accepting that people need each other. The landmark stage of development where the child recognizes his or her own independence is approximately eighteen months, when he or she is highly mobile, has a basic sense of trust, and is starting to plant internally good mental images of significant love objects.

As the child gets to the age of thirty-six months, this autonomy should be set in place by the solidification of the positively introjected mental representation. A "positive introject" is simply a picture inside of a child's mind of a solid and consistent love object.

Independence and autonomy lead to having opinions and the ability to make decisions within our lives. A good sense of independence and autonomy is really knowing that your opinions are valuable, while also knowing that those valuable opinions will not always be the ones chosen to be implemented by those around you.

Children should not be raised with a fierce sense of independence where messages are given that child should not or does not need other people. It is healthier to have a feeling of interdependence and a sense of being okay about being interdependent. The child who can both offer and accept help tends to be the healthy child.

There are children who can offer others help but cannot accept help for themselves, almost as if they do not deserve it. There are also children who can accept help and expect others to serve out of a sense of entitlement but are unable to offer assistance or help to anyone else. These children tend to wear out their peers and end up going from friend to friend, never consistently holding a relationship over time.

The seventh characteristic is the ability to accept responsibilities and cope with problems. Obviously the young child's coping skills grow with age, as long as a significant love object mentors and nurtures the child through development. I observed a marvelous example of this in a kindergarten classroom when on the first day of school the teacher mistakenly wore a left navy shoe and right black shoe. The shoes were similar; however, it was noticeable, especially to the kindergarteners, that they were mismatched. When one of the little girls in the front row pointed out, "Teacher, you have different color shoes on," the teacher responded, "I want this to be the first lesson that everyone learns this year. That lesson is: it is okay in this classroom to make mistakes, because mistakes are for correcting." She was telling these young children not only to accept responsibility but also that lessons are learned from mistakes. (The teacher did say from now on she was going to get dressed with the light on in her bedroom.)

Unfortunately today, many young children are being reared with the fear of accepting responsibility, as if anything that goes wrong is equivalent to making them a bad person. Under this kind of defining the child has to deny any responsibility, which then stunts potential growth in problem-solving ability and hones the capacity to blame others.

The eighth characteristic of good mental health is the ability to give love and to treat others with respect. This characteristic is the cornerstone upon which everything is built. Having the capacity to give love assumes that love was planted within the child and the child perceives himself or herself as lovable. It is impossible to give away something that you do not have. Children who are "love starved" find it difficult to love others because they perceive love like they would a piece of pie: if you share your piece of pie, you are going to get less.

The amount of respect given to people should be equal whether they are three feet tall or six feet tall. I know of few better ways to treat others with respect than to listen. Full and complete attention to the child delivers the message of respect. As the child gets older and more verbal, one of the best tactics to respect others is to talk "nice" about them when they are not there. This holds true with adults also. To improve relationships with other people, respect them verbally and talk positively about them when they are not present. What we say about another person will inevitably get back to that person. If saying positive things is attributed to you, the relationship has really no place to go but to improve.

It also should be noted that when positive things are said about others, whether children or adults, positive mental representations (pictures) are placed in one's own mind representing that person, and the perceptive adult or child will be able to ascertain whether or not there is a positive mental image in the other person's mind. What we say influences what we think, and what we think influences how we act and what kind of cues people pick up from us.

The ninth characteristic of good mental health is the ability to accept one's own feelings and the ability to control those feelings along with the accompanying emotion. I am working with a seventeen-year-old male who was rejected by his birth parents and adopted by another family. This young man has had enough hurt and rejection in his life to turn off his feelings. One of the treatment goals is to allow him to feel and admit that he feels. He has reported to me repeatedly that allowing and accepting his own feelings is terrifying.

His primary feeling is rage because of perceived rejection, and to accept that feeling as a starting point allows him to widen the repertoire of feeling states.

In the children I have treated, if they have shut off feelings of hurt or rejection, they seem also to shut off an equal amount of joy and pleasure. Emotions seem to be on a continuum, complete joy at one end and complete feelings of loss and rage at the other end. When one denies one end of the continuum, both ends seem to head toward the center, until the child has a limited range of feelings or isolates and shuts off feelings altogether. The center of the continuum is zero: no feelings of hurt or rage and no feelings of joy or pleasure.

When one has the ability to accept feelings, it then becomes the task to steer the feelings and the concomitant emotion. It is quite common for children to control others with their emotion in an attempt to control the emotion. Children send their feelings into others and watching other people handle the feelings that they placed on or within them. The ability to control one's emotions is learned through modeling and through adults who are willing to take on and feel some of the child's emotion and thereby metabolize and model how to break down the emotion into its component parts, label the emotion, and find ways to reduce the emotion's intensity or possible destructive power.

This process of breaking down another's emotions can be done with physical exercise as well as good verbalization and rationalization process. Interestingly enough, children are supposed to use adults to learn how to handle their own emotions, and they do that by giving the adult some of their emotion to feel. Watching how the adult handles their emotion and then taking their emotion back is the primary method children use to learn impulse control. That is why it is so important for adults to recognize who "owns" the feelings and that they are being used as a modeling agent for the child's developing coping skills.

The tenth characteristic of good mental health must be the development of one's capacity, interests, and skills for living. Each child needs to recognize what it is he or she does well, even if it is as simple as being able to set the table or pour the milk. It is appropriate to encourage children to associate with other peers who do different things well. A sense of community can be built in a group of children, each having his or her own skills and learning to recognize those skills and offering them as part of a collective group that can work together on projects. In play, each child chooses various skills and with others forms a choir of different talents that is capable of performing and producing wonderful results. The number one reason for "burnout" in adults is a lack of cognitive growth; children also need to grow every day in their physical as well as cognitive skills and delight in the performance that they are able to display.

Good mental health is wonderfully contagious. The bad news is no one can share something he or she does not have. With a conscious effort we could "infect" everyone with good mental health and take joy in observing each other and ourselves grow to our maximum potential.

CHAPTER 2

Attachment

Based on my observations of hundreds of children and hundreds of adults, I believe the interpersonal behaviors of many adults as well as children are inadequate. The question, then, is why some people develop positive interpersonal processes and others do not.

Attachment is a learned process. Human beings invest in other human beings as they have been invested in. People invest themselves as their original caretakers initially invested in them. If a child is not nurtured well or attached well, that lack of knowledge or capacity to invest in another person is flawed. It is not possible to give away something you never had.

So what is good attachment? No single behavior could be identified as good attachment or attachment behavior. The phenomenon of attachment really is a group of behaviors as well as the process or context of those behaviors. Beverly James defines attachment as "a reciprocal, enduring, emotional, and physical affiliation between a child and a caregiver."[2] I would like to expand on this definition by adding that attachment is a reciprocal, enduring investment of physical energy in a real whole person as well as a reciprocal and enduring investment of psychic energy in a real whole person, both currently and in the future in the form of mental representations and expectations.

Attachment is a reciprocal, enduring investment of physical energy; in other words, it takes work. There are things that one must do, a group of behaviors, a nurturing process: touching, talking in a soothing manner, answering distress calls in a brief period of time, etc. When I say "real whole person," it is the capacity to see a person as having both good characteristics and bad characteristics.

In very young children, a mental "splitting" process occurs when infants see the nurturing caregivers as either "all good," because they are responded to and cared for, or "all bad," if their needs are not met and they are responded to harshly or not at all. Under the best of conditions these two feelings (the "all good" caregiver and the "all bad" caregiver) must bond themselves together as the child matures so that the child recognizes that it's possible to love Mommy and be angry and frustrated with her at the same time. This anger and frustration does not send Mommy away or cause her to die, but, because Mommy is consistent, the child is given the message that it is safe to have alternating good and bad feelings toward one person. This helps the child maintain attachments and relationships throughout the rest of the life cycle.

Children who grow into adolescents and adults who have not mastered the capacity to tolerate these opposing good and bad feelings in one person will never sustain a consistent relationship. Therefore in the definition, seeing a "real whole person" is an important aspect of the attachment process and one that has to be a reciprocal process that flows both ways. Not only is there an investment of physical energy *in* another person, there is also an investment of psychic energy or emotional energy *from* the other person.

Emotional energy includes thoughts and feelings, good memories, and the sense that the other person will provide care even during times of stress. Not only must we believe that the attached person will come to our aid at a moment's notice, but we also have to believe that person will be there in times of future duress, and we hold that image in our mind in what is called a mental representation.

Therefore "attachment is a reciprocal, enduring investment of physical energy (doing things—the group of behaviors) in a real whole person (both good and bad) as well as a reciprocal enduring investment of psychic energy (emotional) in a real whole person, both currently and in the future, in the form of mental representations (pictures in our minds) and expectations." This definition is what I might term as the ideal attachment process! This definition views attachment not only as a historical event but also as a current event, as well as a probable future process and event.

There are different kinds of attachment processes; in my practice I have seen three main types. The first is the good attachment process previously described, the second is a trauma bonding, and the third is a dependency type attachment. Let's do a brief explanation of these three types of attachments using figure 1. If we line up on the horizontal line the words *attachment, dependency,* and *trauma bond,* we can vertically describe and compare these three types of bonding. I resist calling all three of these processes actual attachments because in fact the dependency process as well as the trauma bond are not attachment processes or behaviors, but they are powerful bonds that frequently are played out between children and adults as well as between two adults.

Figure 1

Attachment	Dependency	Trauma Bond
Love	Instrumentally reliant	Terror
Takes time	Transient	Instant
Reciprocity	Non-specific	Domination
Person seen as essential for happiness	Getting "fed" is more important than who feeds	Person experienced as essential for survival
Proximity triggers safety and pleasure	Proximity means being by whoever is available	Proximity triggers conflict, alarm, and numbing
Defines "self" as separate person (identity)	I am somehow incomplete	I am an extension of another's needs

| Autonomy and individuation | Whoever you are, love me so I can feel complete | Obedient to the will of others |
| Self-mastery | Immature help seeker | Mastery by others |

In attachment, the primary emotion is love. It is an emotional and physical affiliation and an intense affection. The primary emotion of dependency, on the other hand, is what is known as an instrumentally reliant feeling: love that is based on providing for one's needs. It is reliant on another person or dependent on another person as if that other person were an instrument to be used. The primary emotion in a trauma bond is terror, and emotionally speaking the trauma-bonded child's brain is usually on full alert and at a very high arousal level.[3]

Real attachment takes time to develop and come into its fullness. Attachment involves trust and is based on predictability and on the ability of other people to read personal cues accurately. Once that trust is set in place, attachment really begins to blossom.

Dependency, on the other hand, does not take much time and tends to be transient. Objects are interchangeable, and trust is never really set in place. The dependency bond accepts the changes as long as the need seems to be met.

Trauma bonding takes virtually no time to achieve, because of the extreme threat that often accompanies this type of attaching behavior. As an example of trauma attachment, I once had a child in treatment whose father would shoot and kill small animals in front of the boy in order to demonstrate that his word was law and what the boy observed with the animals could happen to him if he stepped out of line.

Good attachment behavior also is reciprocal. Even in infancy a child will smile, coo, kick appropriately, and express a reciprocal response to a nurturing caregiver. Attachment therefore is a caring two-way reciprocity with specific persons within the child's life who are trusted and predictable.

Dependency, on the other hand, results in non-specific and very general relationships. A salesman who traveled all over the country resided in six different places within the continental United States, living with a different girlfriend in each major sales city. This is the extreme of a dependent type of relationship attachment in that he had a general relationship with each of the women. When I asked him if his California girlfriend liked flowers, he stated, "Oh yes, she loves flowers." Then he added that each of the other women in the different cities also loved flowers. Trying to pin him down as to how well he knew the women, I asked him what kind of flowers the California girlfriend liked specifically. He said that she really liked flowers and that he could send her roses or carnations or orchids or any kind of flowers, because she "likes them all." I offered that my wife specifically liked a bouquet of carnations, red and pink, with baby's breath, to which he responded, "See, your wife likes flowers, too." This man was incapable of grasping the specificity that is needed for a good attachment.

When one attaches to another person, he or she knows that person specifically, in detail, including likes and dislikes. In a trauma bond there is no reciprocity or specificity; there is only domination and fear. The child sees that the other person is powerful and that the child is not, and that is as specific as it gets in the interpersonal process. Domination and fear rule.

In good attachment the attaching person sees the attachment object as essential for happiness. Happiness can be defined as being made up of caring, touching, safety, protection, and nurturance—both physical and emotional. In infancy and in young childhood, attachment is visible, in the sense that children will eat only if Mommy or Daddy or a significant love object feeds them. Who feeds them is much more important than what they are eating or even that they are eating. This is one of the reasons why the eating process is so important. Well-attached children often gaze into the significant love object person's eyes while they are eating and partake not only of food but also of emotional sustenance.

In dependency, getting fed is more important than who does the feeding. A dependent kind of attachment involves worrying about a continual supply of needs being met, and it doesn't matter who meets the needs as long as they are being met. If a child of eight to nine months can be passed around a room of total strangers without exhibiting stranger anxiety, I wonder if the child is attached and whether the child really is developing a dependency survival mode of inter-relationships. Children are supposed to care about a small number of significant love objects, or specific people, within their environment.

In the trauma bond, a person is experienced as essential for survival. The child sees the powerful person as a person who won't feed the child or who will feed the child if the child is submissive. Trauma bonding is a powerful identification with the dominant person, with survival as the theme.

In good attachment, proximity triggers feelings of safety and pleasure. In other words, when the significant love object is around, the child feels safe and able to rest. The very presence of a nurturing person brings on relaxation, safety, and a sense of being cared for.

In a dependent relationship, proximity to any person brings on a wish and a hope to have needs met. There's no one safe person; therefore any person has the potential of becoming safe. Safety gets equated with availability. If someone is available to meet the needs, then the child will feel safe; if no one is available, the child may not feel safe. In good attachment, only specific people bring on that safety feeling.

In trauma bonding, proximity or the closeness of the dominant powerful figure triggers conflict, alarm, and, in children, often a numbing effect. Children often try to remain close to the trauma-bonded dominant person because that person is seen as the "life grantor." It feels much safer for them to stay close to the life grantor, for fear of what would happen to them without that person. Trauma bonding truly is powerful because of the perception that living or dying, surviving or not surviving, is connected to the dominator. When children are around a dominant trauma figure, they may shut off all their emotions and go emotionally numb. This protects them not only from potential physical attacks but also from emotional excitement, which can become unbearable.

Good attachment allows children to define themselves as separate from their nurturing love object. This is seen as okay by the child because of the predictable and consistent nurturing nature of the significantly attached person. When we have an attachment to another person, we will submit willfully to that person out of love, but we still maintain a separate identity and integrity as a whole human being apart from the attachment love object.

A dependent person does not see himself or herself as whole or complete and therefore has to have people around in order to feel strong in society. One young man told me, "I feel so incomplete without my girlfriend. It's almost as if the marbles in my head fit perfectly into the holes in hers." This young man was not attempting to be derogatory about himself or his girlfriend but was trying to make the point that his identity and his selfhood were incomplete without being enmeshed with another human being.

In trauma bonding, the child sees the self as an extension of the powerful person's needs. The child sees that because he or she is an extension, the child could literally be cut off. The child sees himself or herself somewhat as a "parasite" on a host, and left without the host, the child would die. Trauma bonding is truly an unhappy way to live.

Good attachment is also earmarked by autonomy and individuation. Autonomy simply means self-rule, and children quickly learn that in a healthy attachment relationship they have a lot of latitude in terms of what they can do, what they want to do, and what they will do. They can choose to commit or submit to a significant love object or push the person away, at least temporarily, and "do their own thing." Children have often defined this for me as "being real by myself." This process of being an individual does not mean that children can or would want to live without someone that they are attached to, but they are simply exerting a unique sense of identity and completeness within themselves without having to have a host or a feeling of enmeshment.

In a dependency type of relationship, the dependent person will look for love indiscriminately so that he or she can feel complete. There is not much concern about who the other person is as long as the person is available.

In a trauma bond the child has to be obedient to the will of others, therefore precluding autonomy (self-rule) and a sense of individuation. The child has to take on the attitude and position of "slave" for survival.

Good attachment also makes it safe for the child to extend himself or herself and express self-mastery. Because of the love of an attachment figure, the child can go out boldly and experiment, try things out, fail, retreat, and go out again to explore. The child actually self-actuates when "plugged in" with an attachment figure. A wonderful child development paradox exists here in that when we belong, we can venture out on our own.

In dependency, children tend to be immature help-seekers and will move only if they can cling to someone else. They won't extend themselves too far without holding on to someone for reassurance. It's almost as if they do not have the core or the essence of attachment, so they cannot boldly go out and seek new experiences. Dependent persons do not seem to have a solid mental representation or picture of a safe person planted in their heads securely enough for them to actually leave people.

In a trauma bond children believe that their mastery is really not their mastery but is mastery by others. They wait to get moved by the powerful one and tend not to take the risk of exploring or venturing out without explicit permission by the dominant trauma-bonded person.

Understanding how a child thinks and perceives relationships will not only set up an empathic resonance but also help us to discern the most appropriate entrance into the treatment process.

What Good Attachment Does

Good attachment could be likened to an expert conductor who is responsible to orchestrate and integrate all of the various component parts and instruments of an orchestra. Good attachment seems to be the "conductor" that organizes development, emotional responses, and a sense of reality as that person develops within the context of other human beings. I can identify at least fourteen of the various "instruments" that are orchestrated by the attachment conductor.

Good attachment promotes brain and neural development. In an absolutely exquisite book entitled *A General Theory of Love*, the authors state,

The mammalian nervous system cannot self-assemble. Many subsystems of the mammalian brain do not come preprogrammed; maturing mammals need limbic regulation to give coherence to neurodevelopment. Without this general guidance, neural cacophony ensues: behavioral systems are constructed, but without proper harmony between the interdigitating parts.[4]

When a healthy baby is born, the human brain contains everything that it needs. The brain is in fact a relational organ that only develops well as it interacts with other human organisms. This human interaction actually promotes dendrite growth and neural connections.

Good attachment also neutralizes aggression. Good attachment is instrumental in resolving the primary ambivalence of early childhood when twelve- to eighteen-month-old children realize they are not the center of the universe, they are not omnipotent, and they cannot control everyone around them. Well-attached children realize that they are loved and protected; however, they still get extremely indignant over the fact they no longer can be the omnipotent ruler, and they will hang on to the "dynamic duo" feeling that mother and baby have formed. This brings out a great deal of anger and aggression in the child, and because of that good attachment the child can become indignant, can be very angry at the significant love object and at the same time still feel protected and connected to that love object. The attachment is what neutralizes primary rage and aggression.

In the developing unattached child, the aggression does not seem to be neutralized, because of the experience of conditional love and the constant threat of abandonment. This produces a significant amount of early rage in the child, something that we will discuss at length in chapter 13.

Another advantage of good attachment is that it promotes frustration tolerance. Every child in the developmental process needs to learn to wait. Good attachment offers the young child both a model and a "soothing mechanism" in the form of an attached person. This attached person helps modulate the emotion of frustration in the young child, shares in the intensity of having to forestall needs and wants, and lends ego to the child via sharing of the child's feelings. The sharing of feelings between the primary attachment figure and the child is in fact a substitution for the child acting out and demanding or even fighting to get needs or wants met immediately. As any mother can tell you, the child will wait and be able to tolerate that frustration much better when a significantly attached person stands with the child, maybe even touches the child or holds the child in the process of waiting. This process promotes the ability to hold oneself when the frustration of delay (which is inevitable in this world) is presented to the child.

A fourth advantage of good attachment is that it promotes the tolerance of ambivalence. Good attachment actually makes it okay to feel two contrasting feelings at the same time toward one person. The child could be furious with the mother for not complying with his or her immediate wishes but at the same time feel great love for the mother. Between the ages of eighteen months and three years, every child needs to learn to be able to feel love and anger toward one person at the same time.

In the workshops that I give for young adults and adolescents, I tell them that unless they have learned the capacity to tolerate ambivalence, they will never stay married. In a marriage relationship one of the most important characteristics the human being has to possess is the capacity to tolerate ambivalence. The capacity to tolerate ambivalence actually promotes the ability to sustain a long-term relationship, which of course is a rudimentary component of good attachment.

Another advantage of good attachment is that it builds the ability to trust other people. In my discussion with preschoolers I often ask a child how he knows his mother or his father really loves him. I had one insightful five-year-old answer, "My name is safe on his lips." What this youngster meant was that even though his dad could become angry with him, his dad would not verbally rip him to shreds or mock him mercilessly. A good attachment builds the ability to trust people and is based on consistency and predictability over time. When the process of good attachment has been integrated and learned by the child, it can be transferred to other people, and trusting relationships can be sustained.

Some preschool and kindergarten teachers say to me, "I'm only going to have these children for nine months; why should I establish a significant relationship with any one child?" My standard answer is that it is important to teach them behavior that constitutes good attachment. The process of establishing that attachment through consistent, predictable, nurturing behavior is then *transferable* to the next teacher in the child's progression and will set that child up to learn and feel safe. Many children today have difficulty with basic trust because there has not been that kind of predictable, consistent touching and nurturing that they so need for the process of development. Teachers must teach the process!

Good attachment also builds self-esteem. The development of self-esteem starts at a very early age. The tiny infant is developing self-esteem by the type of response that is given, the predictability over time, and the verbal and physical responses that are felt. If the child experiences responses that are sure and predicable over time, regardless of whether or not he or she is a "difficult" child, the sense of value and self-esteem is greatly enhanced. Good attachment is unconditional. The child does not have to perform and does not have to maintain an intrinsic value in order to be loved and kept by the parent.

Another advantage of good attachment is that it helps promote reality testing. When the child feels safe in the interaction with an attached person, the child can accept making mistakes, knowing that his or her well-attached person will not abandon or reject him or her. The child also differentiates "me" from "not me." By this I mean that the child knows what his or her skills are and what he or she can do solo as opposed to what will require help. The child can also take responsibility to make corrections and to explore farther because of connectedness or attachment. If a child feels secure in attachment, the primitive defense mechanism of denial is not utilized nearly to the extent that an unattached child depends on it.

The child also feels safe to ask questions, the most famous of which are the "why" questions, in the process of understanding the world. The child is testing reality, attempting to integrate and put things together in a mental understanding of how the world functions. This reality testing only happens well when the child feels safe enough to do that in a well-attached environment. The unattached child seems to build many more fearful fantasies of what might happen than the well-attached child does.

The eighth gift of good attachment is that it establishes boundaries within the child. One of the paradoxes of development is that one human being cannot truly be close with another human being without good boundaries. Boundaries include social boundaries, emotional boundaries, verbal boundaries, and spatial boundaries, as well as what I refer to as "stuff" boundaries: respecting physical possessions. The establishment of boundaries is an interactional process best learned within the context of good attachment. It should also be noted that closeness with another human being could be a bit scary unless boundaries are intact, because of the fear of enmeshment: the process of two organisms being so close together that they merge with each other, making it difficult to differentiate one from the other.

The human organism seems to have a fear of abandonment (being left out) as well as the fear of enmeshment. Children see enmeshment as another form of loss and abandonment in the sense that they are not recognized as individual persons and are seen only as an extension or piece of another organism. The establishment of boundaries therefore is essential in the attachment process once the child develops enough cognitive processing (usually around eighteen months) to recognize that the wonderful hands that change diapers and provide food are not the hands connected to the child's body.

Good attachment therefore is closeness with boundaries. This represents a safety in intimacy and a true sense of one's own value and identity. Good boundaries are only established within the context of good attachment relationships. Unattached or poorly attached children may continuously violate another child's boundaries because they crave intimacy and closeness but do not understand that one can have these wonderful characteristics and still maintain a sense of self.

In the treatment of poorly attached adolescents I have experienced the adolescent attaching very closely to me as a therapist to the point of enmeshment. By being as available to the child as humanly possible and by responding predictably and consistently, I enable adolescents to settle down emotionally and work to establish their own sense of self, no longer wanting to "climb into my skin" in order to feel safe. Trust then develops.

Along with the establishment of boundaries comes the promotion of healthy identity formation. This is another advantage of good attachment and has to do with an acceptance of who we are. This includes sexual identity acceptance as well as role acceptance. The role of son or daughter or the role of child versus adult is an accepted process within the context of good attachment. The child develops skills and behaviors that are valued and applauded by the attachment figures, demonstrating to the child a sense of healthy identity. Identity grows within the context of feeling safe and within the freedom that parents give their children by insisting on rules. Identity and safety go hand in hand.

I once had a young man around the age of fourteen come in for treatment because he could not get along with his peers or his teachers. Although he was reluctant to come and talk to a therapist, he came in and flopped down into one of my chairs. He crossed his arms and stated that he didn't want to be in therapy and he was not going to talk to me. I asked the young man to tell me a little about himself, at which point he decided to unconsciously let me know the problem by stating "I can do anything I want."

"What do you mean you can do anything you want?" I asked.

He looked at me and stated rather sarcastically, "Are you deaf? I told you I could do anything I want."

I decided to test this out by asking, "You mean if you wanted to stay out late, your parents would let you do that?"

He stated, "Of course I can stay out late. In fact, if I don't want to come home at all I don't have to."

He was telling the truth; his parents were permissive enough to allow him to stay out all night if he so chose. I then asked him if he could drink beer. He looked at me and stated, "You don't really listen very well for a therapist, do you? I told you I could do anything. If I want to drink a beer, I will simply go into the refrigerator where my dad has his beer, get a can, and drink it, and I can do this in front of him."

By this time my mouth was dropping open, and I expressed my great surprise that he had this much latitude in his process of "learning how to be human." I then looked at him intently and asked, "What do you think about parents who allow their only son, who is fourteen years old, to do absolutely anything he wants to?"

I waited in silence for at least sixty seconds, and I started to see tears rolling down this young man's cheeks. Then he said in a timid voice, "I think parents who let their child do anything he wants do not love him." This child's identity, his sense of self, and his value as a person based itself on good attachment, which also means the safety of rules.

Good attachment also helps to establish impulse control by neutralizing aggression. When a good attachment figure is available, the child uses that figure through a process called "projective identification." Impulses can be modified and brought into control within the context of an attachment figure. An attachment figure is committed enough to the child that intense feelings of the child are first filtered through the more mature attachment figure. It's as if the attachment figure says, "Let me take your feelings and show you how to respond without impulsively getting yourself into trouble." The well-attached child therefore entrusts the loving attachment figure with strong emotions so the attachment figure can demonstrate the process of how to handle these emotions. Impulse control is one of those essential processes that each child needs to develop in order to interact well in school or any other context that requires intentional action.

The well-attached child will also generally develop a capacity for empathy way beyond that of a poorly attached child. Attachment figures share feelings with the child and in fact validate via the listening process that what the child feels is real. The child is then able to say to himself or herself, "I know what I feel is real because you feel it also within our relationship." The child feels heard, listened to, accepted, and valued; therefore the child has the context within which to grow a real empathy and the ability to feel what other people feel. Empathy can only develop well within the context of a safe, consistent attachment figure.

Good attachments also encourage exploration with appropriate risk-taking and without excess fear. Children feel a sense of freedom when the attachment is strong and the love object is internalized. Good attachment assumes the existence of the external safe person on the inside in the form of a mental representation (picture), a voice, a touch, and a feeling of general safety. Fear comes from feeling alone, abandoned, betrayed, and a general sense of unsafeness.

At the age of twenty-three I desperately wanted to go to graduate school and obtain my master's degree in clinical social work. This meant that I would have to move my wife, a newborn baby, and what few earthly possession I had to Ann Arbor, Michigan, because I had been accepted at the University of Michigan graduate school. This was a huge move for us and brought on extreme anxiety over how we would live for the next two years in a city where neither one of us knew a soul.

The day we left to move to Ann Arbor, my widowed mother pulled into our driveway just seconds before we were ready to pull out. She looked me directly in the eye and stated, "Phillip, I know you are very nervous and anxious about this move. I also know you are doing the right thing, and I am one hundred percent behind you. I want you to know if you ever, ever have need of anything, I want you to give me a call, and I guarantee you that whatever it is you need, I will make sure that you have it within twenty-four hours." I left Grand Rapids, Michigan, that day with a sense of security and an internal picture that will last a lifetime. With that kind of physical as well as emotional backup, any young person can obtain the freedom to extend himself or herself and take risks.

Good attachment also defines for the child the terms *love, hate,* and *nothing.* It's obvious why *love* is defined within a good attachment, but *hate* is also defined well within a good attachment. The child has the freedom to intensely dislike and even have hostility toward people without the fear of being utterly and completely abandoned. Within the context of good attachment, children will not feel the full terror of nothingness; however, because they are well loved they also have the capacity to acknowledge and understand others who are not. Good attachment therefore also banishes what I term "the terrible nothingness."

There is a most exquisite movie that children used to enjoy ten or more years ago entitled *The Neverending Story.*[5] In this movie a little boy loses his mother to death and then has to negotiate his development with a father who is loosely attached to him, making the process even more traumatic. The youngster has to battle against the ominous "terrible nothingness" that chases him throughout the movie, and he must turn to other people and figures to help him negotiate the passage of development.

The one thing that children fear the most is "nothing." There is not a child that I have met in over thirty-five years of work with children who wouldn't rather be hated or abused if they could not be loved. The reason children would choose such treatment is that if they are abused they're at least being acknowledged and often touched, albeit brutally. What children cannot tolerate is being utterly and completely left alone in a state of nothingness. It is paradoxical that children fear "nothing" most, but most adults have this exact same fear, and most adults would choose the life of trouble rather than a life filled with nothing.

Good attachment is absolutely essential for good development, and good attachment promotes and builds and integrates all of the other structures within the brain and the social context that children find themselves in.

In the next chapter we will take a look at a process of normal development in more detail and in simple terms watch how the child spends at least eighteen months feeling attached and then eighteen months learning to feel separate. These are two very important developmental phases for the child and a process that must be sequential in nature in order for the child to emerge as an integrated whole adult.

CHAPTER 3

Perceptions of Normal Development

The minute the male sperm implants itself in the female egg and fertilizes it, the process of child development begins. Within hours of this fertilization the female body makes numerous biochemical changes that virtually go unnoticed until the female misses her menstrual cycle. Because of the biochemical changes, extremely subtle changes in the woman's behavior begin to happen.

On two separate occasions I was engaged in play therapy with three-year-olds, following a theme that revolved around safety and the fear of being hurt or losing significant people. Rather dramatically in both cases, the three-year-olds switched their play to that of nurturing caregiving, and obvious baby themes entered into the process. Because of the dramatic switch in play I shared that observation with each mother and asked each of them whether she was pregnant. In both cases the mothers were surprised and stated they did not think so, but in both cases the mothers returned a week later saying they were pregnant.

The mothers were a bit "spooked" over the fact that their own children were able to process through their play that they knew their mothers were pregnant before the mothers themselves knew. I explained to the mothers that their children were not psychic, but that rapid changes within the female body once fertilization takes place cause mothers to emit subtle changes in the way they interact with their existing child. Young children are extremely perceptive to reading cues on an unconscious basis and start to demonstrate themes of nurturing, feeding, touching, holding, wrapping things, and unwrapping in the process of their play. The three-year-olds do not in fact know what they are saying via their play; however they certainly perceive the differences within the nurturing process between their mothers and themselves. In both cases these mothers gained new respect and appreciation for how precisely their preschoolers could read their moods, temperaments, and behaviors.

The developmental process starts very early, and nurturing a young child actually begins in the prenatal period, in four specific ways.

First, it is important for expectant mothers to care for themselves physically, including exercise and staying motorically active. Exercise and activity in that prenatal period tend to keep anxiety and depression at bay during this period of rapid change. Mothers would do well to keep down excessive stimulation during this prenatal period so that the body's stress hormones are kept at a low level.

A good diet and plenty of water are other important physical nurturing that should happen during this period of development. In his discussion of the importance of water, Eric Jensen states that 75 percent of Americans are chronically dehydrated, and in 37 percent of Americans the thirst mechanism is so weak it is often mistaken for hunger.[6]

Mothers often stroke themselves by rubbing their tummies as if they are massaging the baby in uterus. This prenatal period actually is a maternal self-nurturing process that then translates into a mother-child nurturing process.

The second aspect of the prenatal nurturing process has to do with verbal communication. It is important for both mother and father to talk regularly to the baby as the child develops. When a father and mother talk with each other and directly to their baby in the womb, at birth the infant is able to recognize both the mother's and the father's voices.

The third aspect of prenatal nurturing has to do with social-emotional nurturing and support from the extended family. This aids the whole process of bonding, which starts prior to the baby being born. Bonding is helped by having a "wanted" full-term baby where there are two parents looking forward to the birth and a supportive family around these parents, who all place a value on the child. This helps to keep stress levels low and sets up a higher probability that there will be a good reciprocal mother-child interaction and that the responses from the newborn baby will be picked up as "readable" cues. The social-emotional stability during this period means having people around who can help regulate the parents and thereby keep the mother and father on an emotional equilibrium, particularly during the last trimester of the pregnancy.

The fourth area has to do with the cognitive development of the fetus. In developmental charts it is interesting to note that it is around day twenty-two from the time of fertilization when neural folds begin to fuse into what will become the baby's brain and brain stem. To enhance cognitive development, mothers need to stay away from medications, drugs, and alcohol. Barring genetic anomalies, the baby then has a good possibility of developing all of the normal brain structures intact.

Part of the prenatal nurturing process also has to do with the fantasies that the mother and father have of the expected baby. It is important that both the mother and father develop a mental picture of what kind of child they will have, even so far as the skills and traits the child will develop. This fantasy image of the baby (even though it may not turn out to be accurate) will help the mother and father make the child feel "real," which is part of the infant feeling valuable. The prenatal nurturing period sets the stage for later nurturing tendencies.

I particularly like the way Margaret Mahler has laid out the various stages of development. Her perspective has helped me conceptualize how important each stage is. When I see difficulties later in life, Mahler's chart also helps to delineate and pinpoint where the process of development may have gone awry.[7]

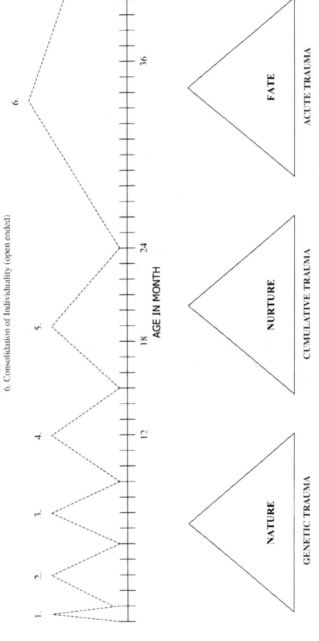

STAGE OF DEVELOPMENT
(M.S. Mahler)

1. Normal Autistic Phase (1st month)
2. Normal Symbiotic Phase (1 - 4 months)
3. Differentiation Phase (4 - 9 months)
4. Practicing Phase (9 - 15 months)
5. Rapprochement Phase (15 - 24 months)
6. Consolidation of Individuality (open ended)

AGE IN MONTH

NATURE   NURTURE   FATE

GENETIC TRAUMA   CUMULATIVE TRAUMA   ACUTE TRAUMA

Mahler calls the first month of the infant's life outside of the womb the "normal autistic phase," meaning the baby starts to formulate its own perceptions and fantasies of what the real world is like. Babies are taking in information at such a rapid pace, however, that at times they need to shut down and attempt to block stimuli in order to rest and regroup. In this first month in a normally developing child one will readily be able to observe what Mahler calls the baby's "normal stimulus barrier." This is a process that the baby uses to filter out excessive stimuli and process emotion along with its intensity. In that first month of life babies are trying to figure out how safe they are; therefore they need a stimulus barrier in order to enhance their own feeling of safety.

Mothers should provide additional stimulus barriers for the child. It is inappropriate for mothers to be carting around two-day-old infants in a busy shopping mall where the extra stimulation of lights, noise, and jostling touch are frequent occurrences. Mothers do not have to hibernate themselves for the first month of the infant's life, but when mothers act as an additional stimulus barrier the child initially builds a better perception of the environment as being safe and inviting rather than over-stimulating and dangerous.

Within that first month of life my granddaughter demonstrated good abilities to screen out excessive stimulation by simply turning her head and refusing to acknowledge the person playing with her. After I engaged in play with her for several minutes, suddenly she would turn her head, avert her eyes from mine, and almost "play dead." I recognized this as her natural "rest cycle" and her need to cut down on stimulation. I learned that the appropriate thing to do was simply hold the child in silence. Allowing children to rest and protect themselves from stimulation is as important as giving children appropriate stimulation for their developmental process.

The second phase of development that Mahler talks about is the normal symbiotic phase. The word *symbiosis* means two living organisms in close proximity, almost to the point of being perceived as one organism. In other words, the mother and child in the symbiotic period form such a duo unity within one common boundary that the baby may literally believe that he or she has four wonderful hands: two hands that he or she flails around and attempts to control, and two hands that take care of him or her. There is certainly an awareness of a need-satisfying object: Mother. Mother and baby form an omnipotent system.

This normal symbiotic phase is absolutely vital for development, because a major portion of trust develops during this phase. Trust develops because of the caregiver's predictability, dependability, and constant availability. The mother has positive expectations that the child is growing well, and the baby has positive expectations that he or she will be cared for down to the minutest detail.

Mahler describes a rhythm or a choreography that happens, like a dance between mother and child. The dance is the baby expressing a need and the mother responding at the appropriate time with the appropriate measure. When the needs are met and when the baby feels calm, the world is good and basic trust starts to develop and flourish. This basic trust is important because it is transferable to other significant love objects, such as Dad, Grandpa, Grandma, and other people the child contacts. When Mom and Dad are trustworthy, the baby's assumptions are that most other people are trustworthy too. (Unfortunately the converse is also true.)

During this stage the baby develops the feeling and sensation that he or she is safe because he or she is fed, changed, talked to, and protected. Under these conditions the child sees himself or herself as "good." The child feels as if he or she is a good baby because of the predictable and dependable responses from the significant caregiver. In those first four months of life a significant portion of self-esteem and self-image is developed in the young child. The development of self-esteem is not something that starts at age five when the child hits public education or can recite the alphabet. The development of self-esteem starts within days after the baby's birth.

The next phase of development is the differentiation phase, which starts at about four months of age and extends to about nine months of age. The child starts to develop a sense of body image and begins reading people's cues at a rapid rate. The bodies of young children are "big deals" to the child, which is why it is essential that the child be touched appropriately and mirrored appropriately by the significant caregiver.

Mirroring the child refers to the type of expression that the adult gives the child whenever the child performs a new skill or activity, often wanting to show the parent. I remember one of my grandchildren starting to walk by hanging on to furniture at about the age of eight and a half months. Every step she took she would turn around and look directly into my eyes. She wanted to be mirrored. The mirroring response that I gave to her was a huge smile, an encouraging word, and twinkling eyes. I even gestured with my hands as if I was clapping wildly. When children are mirrored in such a manner, their performance, who they are, and their bodies are infused with value. Pride develops, as well as a lot of what Stanley Greenspan calls "intentional communication."[8] These children want to connect, so they observe others and delight in personal performance.

The next phase is called the differentiation phase by Mahler because the child is leaning that he or she is a separate entity "differentiated" from the significant caregiver. Cognitively children are continuing to develop and recognize that the hands that change them, feed them, and protect them are actually not their own.

By eight months of age children fully recognize who their significant love objects are and develop what is called "stranger anxiety." Stranger anxiety is the earmark of a child developing significant relationships and close attachments. Children by the age of eight or nine months who exhibit no stranger anxiety whatsoever concern me. These children simply look for whatever they can get from whomever is holding them but do not demonstrate significant love attachment to one human. A child who exhibits stranger anxiety generally has significant attachment.

At this phase the child also exhibits lots of emotions, some of which require a caregiver who is able to regulate the child's negative emotions. Young children at this age have both engagement cues—gestures and babblings and eye contact that draw people closer to them—and disengagement cues, behaviors that push people away or stop others from stimulating them. The parent's job is to respect and accept disengagement cues as well as accept and respond to engagement cues. The parent also needs to provide and model ways for children to soothe themselves, whether it's through soft touch, warm blankets, or nurturing food. One soothing technique I heartily endorse is reading books to children, starting at the age of four months and continuing until the child indicates that he or she is no longer interested in this type of activity with the parent.

The next Mahler developmental phase is called the practicing phase. This extends from approximately nine months of age to fifteen months of age. During this phase of development the child continues the differentiation process and starts to use Mother or the significant caregiver in different ways. Rather then wanting to stay close to Mother, the child moves away and uses Mom as a home base. The child starts to walk, and because the child has a secure home base and a nurturing mother, the child moves out away from Mother and may even do things in another room, only to come back often to check on where Mom is and what she is doing.

During this phase of development the child needs lots of "refueling" and metaphorically uses Mother as a "gas station," with Mother dispensing soothing emotion and reassurance that everything will be all right. The child then plays at a distance away from Mother or may even extend out to approach other people, always knowing where that refueling station is so that, should the child run out of fuel, he or she can go back and "fill up."

It is not unusual to see a twelve- to fifteen-month-old child use the mother's lap as a repository for a box of blocks. The child will pick out a block from a box across the room and deliver it to the lap of the waiting mother. The child then heads back, repeats the process with another block, and continues until the box of blocks on the other side of the room is empty. In that way the child is actually practicing to be separate and away from the mother while at the same time acting like a yo-yo, always bouncing back to the mother. It is important then that mothers give their children a sense of connection. They can do this with eye contact, gestures, or body position. Mothers give out the message "I see you and I can be there in a flash if you need me."

Because children are practicing to "be themselves," narcissism is at its peak. The child is now walking and loves his or her body's ability to move. The child will learn problem-solving techniques, such as walking over to Mom, grabbing her hand, and pulling her to an object out of the child's reach. The child still has plenty of leftover feelings of omnipotence and still generally sees himself or herself as the center of the universe. The narcissism that the child has at this age actually helps the child to regulate a sense of self-esteem, which goes hand-in-hand with the capacity to problem-solve.

During this phase the child is also learning how to regulate or modulate emotions and does so in imitation and role-playing. It is not unusual to see a fifteen-month-old child spanking a doll vigorously to the shock of parents who know they do not treat that child in the manner that the child is treating the baby doll. In this way, however, the child is learning to regulate anger and physical impulses.

In this practicing stage, the child will still need to have control over Mom's leaving. The child can move away, but Mom can only move away with the child's permission. Cognitively the child starts to recognize that he or she can manipulate objects and people, and to a degree this is okay. Generally children who are genuinely loved and well nurtured are able to accept structure and even the word "no," although they may fuss a bit. It is the child who does not have the power of love that will tenaciously hang on to the love of power and manipulation.

The next phase of development, according to Mahler, is rapprochement. From fifteen months to approximately twenty-four months the child, after practicing moving away from the mother, now must resolve the fact that in a world with other people, the child is no longer going to be allowed to be the center of the universe and the omnipotent dictator of the world. The child therefore moves away from significant love objects, gets angry at them, and then moves back toward them and wants to be nurtured. Fifteen minutes later the child wants to push significant love objects away and again demands to be the ruler, only to become a bit frightened and again return to the nurturing love object.

This back and forth scenario happens a great deal during this stage of development; hence the name *rapprochement.* It is a rediscovery of Mother as a separate individual and a new awakening of a goal-directed anger, which of course includes the magic word "no." The child learns to deal with the reality and the frustration that reality brings and is often extremely indignant over "big people" not allowing him or her to run the world. There are many periods of indecision and emotional extreme for the child.

During this phase of development there is often what Mahler calls the "rapprochement crisis," where the child learns to accept intense conflicting feelings toward one person. This is called *intense ambivalence,* and children at this stage learn that they can be extremely angry at their parents and love them dearly at the same time. This is an extremely important lesson, and parents also need to model the ability to tolerate these conflicting emotions. This is one of the reasons young children watch their moms and dads so closely. Can Mommy love Daddy and be angry at Daddy at the same time?

During this stage the child also discovers sexual differences and is curious about genital differences and male-female characteristics.

Right in the middle of this developmental phase—at approximately eighteen to twenty months—is when the child emotionally switches from learning to attach to learning to be separate. Between the ages of zero and eighteen months the child's primary duty and task is to learn how to attach to significant love objects. By eighteen to twenty months these love objects should be securely set in place in the child's mind as well as within the child's immediate environment. The child then is free to start to learn, as Mahler says, to "individuate," which means to develop a distinct personality. From about eighteen to twenty months all the way to thirty-six months, the child learns to be separate and a unique individual, so that by the age of thirty-six months the child feels solidly connected to significant human objects and is ready to extend himself or herself into the "real world." Even though within the first eighteen months the child is learning to attach and in the next eighteen months the child learns to be separate, good parents know that they are never to be far away, so that they can protect the child and provide the child with safety if needed. Noted child psychologist Erna Furman used to say,

"A mother's job is to be there to be left, always available so as not to be needed."

Also in this rapprochement period the child begins to demonstrate what would be called a conscience and becomes sensitive to approval and disapproval. The unattached child does not develop a conscience or the wish to be approved of by significant persons, because there are no people who are significantly attached.

One also sees in this stage a reoccurrence of stranger reactions, because even though the child is learning to be separate, the child is aware that he or she does not want significantly attached people to be far away.

This stage also includes the proverbial temper tantrums, which are signals that the child is indignant over being demoted from king or queen to prince or princess. It is important that, after a tantrum, parents accept and reassure the child. A parent who rejects a child's desire to depend on the parent even after a tantrum raises a fragile person.

From approximately twenty months to forty-eight months the child is learning how to be alone, which really is a curious paradox, because the child would be terrified if in fact significantly loved objects would leave the child utterly alone. This rapprochement phase is a huge developmental phase and one that demands that parents be tolerant, acceptant and readily available, exhibit the wisdom of Solomon, and have the capacity to forgive themselves for continuously making mistakes. This particular phase of development is often as frustrating for the developing child as it is for the parent!

The last phase of Mahler's phases is consolidation of individuality. This phase starts at about twenty-four months and extends to thirty-six months and actually beyond. The next fifteen years past thirty-six months represent to the developing child a reworking of the milestones in the first three years and an attempt to fix any particular one that was not properly set in place. This phase of development does exactly what the title implies: that is, it consolidates the child into a separate individual and starts to help him or her become an interactive part of human relationships. In this phase children develop a stable sense of self boundaries and recognize that their emotions are not what others feel. Their bodies are different from other bodies, their thoughts are not necessarily what someone else may think, and their level of closeness and proximity may differ from people around them.

The child develops huge strides in cognitive processing and complex thought because verbal communication develops rapidly, replacing gestural and emotional language expressions. The child is more tuned in to a time orientation and is able to test out reality by asking the perpetual "why" question. Frustration tolerance rapidly increases, problem solving increases, and the child is able to tie thoughts and feelings into consequences and logical sequence. The child then creates emotional ideas and loves modeling and imitating, particularly the significant adults around him or her.

By thirty-six months the child should have and carry on the inside the pictures of his or her well-attached significant loved persons. In other words, by thirty-six months of age the child knows who really loves him or her and can carry a picture of that person around in his or her mind. At times three-year-old children actually talk to the significantly loved person in the absence of that person, to call forth from the imagination the security of that protective love object. Thirty-six months is a great age for starting a preschool experience because the child should have object constancy well established by this time (object constancy meaning a solid picture of that person in the child's mind and a conviction that the person will not leave or disappear).

There are obviously many more significant developmental issues, but I wanted to give the reader a thumbnail sketch of development from zero to thirty-six months as this will set the stage for chapters later in the book where rage reactions and poor attachment will be defined. To me, the striking thing about the development process is the often paradoxical nature of development; therefore I would like to spend time talking about child development paradoxes.

CHAPTER 4

The Paradoxes of Child Development

Webster's New College Dictionary defines *paradox* as "a seemingly contradictory statement that may nonetheless be true." All of child development is absolutely replete with paradoxes. Through my career I have identified more than thirty, but there are a dozen that may help to explain the developmental process more fully. I will refer to these paradoxes in future chapters, especially as we talk about ways to be helpful for children who are dealing with problems.

Paradox #1: "To get a child to separate, encourage the child to cling."

Separation anxiety in the very young child can be cured in a relatively short period of time by encouraging the child to cling. In other words, for six weeks the mother should encourage the child to do everything with her (at least as much as is feasible) and to constantly let the child know what is about to happen in terms of any events. The mother is to hold the child's hand, sit by the child, and generally be as tolerant as possible of encouraging this child to be by Mother.

This is an attempt to fill the child with the mother. Part of this "fill up" is planting the mother within the child's brain in the form of vivid mental pictures, smells, touches, and interactions. The child has to build up a memory bank of experiences and feelings to convince himself or herself that he or she knows the mother very well. Once this child is confident that he or she knows the mother and has her planted firmly on the inside, the child is then free to let the mother go and start to extend himself or herself into the environment without the close proximity of Mom. A clinging process and putting Mom on the inside is the absolute essential ingredient for letting Mother go.

Paradox #2: "To let go of someone, put the person on the inside."

This paradox is similar to the previous paradox in that in order to let go of someone, there has to be real internal attachment, at least to the mental representation of that person if not to his or her physical body. I recall one particular child therapy case where a baby was removed from the home for severe neglect and spent almost three years in foster care with one consistent caregiver. The child bonded well with the foster parents, as did the foster parents with the child. The foster parents attempted to adopt the child; however, the child's birth father fought a legal battle, and ultimately the child was returned to the home of the birth father and his new wife. These were people whom this child had not known at all for the first three years of life, and the birth father and his new wife wanted desperately to be able to bond with this child.

After being removed from the foster home, the child was obsessed with wondering where his foster parents were, what they were doing, and why they allowed him to move into this strange new home. (It was even in another state.) This young child obviously needed to go through a mourning process, but the adults in this particular case did not understand that. The birth father and new mother decided to get rid of any reminder of the child's foster home and foster parents. They would not discuss the foster home, they would not discuss the foster parents, and they did not allow any pictures or scrapbooks from the previous placement. The child responded with a myriad of behavioral problems, severe temper tantrums, and an eating disorder. By the time the parents came to therapy for this child, both the parents and this child were beside themselves.

I suggested to the new parents that the child would succeed in bonding and in attaching to them if they would allow the child to internalize the previous parents, who were nurturing and loving for the first three years of his life. They got out the old scrapbooks, even a couple of old VCR movies they had of the foster parents, and started to discuss the child's previous "parents." The young child went into a mourning process for his "lost parents" and was visibly sad and depressed. His new parents were able to support and comfort the child while continuing to let the child talk about his previous parents.

After a few months the child started to regain alertness, spontaneity, and pleasure in interactions. This continued, and the child appropriately compartmentalized in "memory boxes" the previous parents and was able to relegate them to those special memory boxes in his brain. He was then able to move ahead with the new relationships and develop attachments.

Paradox #3: "To feel joy you must be able to feel pain."

Over the years I have worked with a number of children who have been severely neglected, abused, and abandoned. One of the available defense mechanism these children have is to deny hurt and to turn off feelings. Psychologically this is called "isolation of affect," and although the child is then impervious to pain, this is done at a cost!

Feelings seem to be on a large continuum. At one end of the continuum are extreme joy and the ability to feel pleasure. At the other end of the continuum are extreme pain, feelings of hurt, and emotional terror. When children start to turn off feelings of pain and hurt, an equal amount of their capacity to feel joy seems also to be inhibited. It's as if both ends of the continuum are inextricably connected, so that when one moves, the other moves also. Children, for the most part, do not turn off joy; however they certainly attempt to reduce or eliminate the feeling and sensation of emotional pain.

The midpoint of the continuum might be called anhedonia, affectlessness, or loss of feeling. Let's imagine there are one hundred increments on one side of the midpoint, all the way to extreme joy, and one hundred increments on the other side, all the way to extreme pain. If the child shuts off the far fifty increments of pain, my observation is that the far fifty increments of extreme joy are also brought toward the midline. The child then has a limited range of feelings, from just a little pain to just a little joy. The further they bring the pain toward the middle, the less joy they are capable of feeling or exhibiting. If a child in fact shuts off all the pain and brings all feelings almost to the midline of "feelinglessness," the child appears with a very restricted range of emotional display. These children often speak in a monotone voice, they lack mobility and facial expression, and they present a rather lifeless, apathetic countenance. The wonderfully adaptive human being has the capability of shutting pain off, but the price of doing so is an equal amount of shutting off of joy and pleasure.

Paradox #4: "If you want a child to share, stress boundaries and ownership."

A kindergarten child brought into class a superhero action figure given to him by his dad. It was his pride and joy, and he wanted to show it to the other children and his teacher. When the other kids saw it, a "kindergarten grab fest" ensued. The owner of the action figure was losing control and started to scream and cry.

The teacher walked over to the group of boys, held out her hand, and demanded the action figure. The teacher then gave a marvelous lesson in teaching this particular child development paradox. She looked at the group of boys and asked, "Whose action figure is this?"

The owner of the action figure stated it was his; it was brand new, and he brought it just to show the other children at school.

The teacher then handed the action figure to the owner and turned to the rest of the group and stated, "That is Jimmy's action figure; he owns it, and you may not touch it without his permission."

The teacher then walked away from the little group, and as she glanced back she could see Jimmy saying to the group as he handed the action figure over to another child, "Here, do you want to play with it?"

The child was able to share his prized action figure only when ownership was recognized and boundaries were drawn explicitly. In order to let something go, you have to have confidence in the ownership and know that ownership is going to be protected, not only by you, but also by those around you.

Paradox #5: "If you are truly attentive to children when you are with them, they will manage with less of you."

I have a bumper sticker that reads "Wherever you are, be there." The message is that being with someone requires a total presence. Dorothy Briggs, in her book *Your Child's Self-Esteem*,[9] talks about an "all hereness" that we should exhibit when interacting with children. The capacity to listen closely, to stay focused, and to give a child full attention truly is a developed skill. When the child feels as if he or she really has you—not just your body, but your whole mind and emotional system as well—the child feels heard. Children need emotional fuel. If children only get a few drops of fuel, they must follow you around and constantly fill their tanks in order to keep going and producing. When a person gives a child full and undivided attention, the child's fuel tank of emotional need quickly starts to fill up.

I tell preschool teachers to start the year with no less than a thousand Band-Aids in the cupboard, and I encourage them to make a big deal over every injury, scrape, or bump the children get. One teacher told me of a child who received a paper cut that was so minute that it could barely be seen with a magnifying glass. The child was crying and carrying on, and the teacher admitted to me she was tempted to tell the child to "toughen up." However, she remembered our previous discussion about this paradox and dutifully got out the Band-Aids, the peroxide and the washcloths and summoned up her own empathic capacities to fully attend to this child. She stated that she could see in the child's face a growing sense of value, and she remarked, "I didn't hear from that child for the rest of the morning except his occasional glance at me and smile."

Paradox #6: "If you want a child to act independently, give that child permission to ask for help."

It seems in our American society that we want children to become independent rapidly. We want them to develop self-help skills and quickly be able to take care of themselves. Most children attempt diligently to comply with the adult's wishes in this regard, but the struggle for independence is greatly enhanced by permission to ask for help and sometimes permission to make a small and temporary regression.

A precocious and highly verbal little girl moved into the state of Michigan with her parents from the south. Her father had landed a good job, and they moved into a very nice house and were able to purchase many pieces of new furniture. One of the moves that the parents made was to fold up the child's crib that she had been sleeping in and to get her a "big girl bed" for the new house in Michigan.

They came to see me approximately three weeks after they had set up their home and, with very dark circles under their eyes, reported that their daughter had not slept through the night for the previous three weeks. We talked about the large move that they made from their old house, from their old state, from their old neighborhood, and from all of their old friends. These parents were loving and nurturing and fully understood that this was a big move for their young daughter. When I found out that they had changed her bed, I suggested that they give their daughter the option of going back to sleeping in her crib.

The parents were visibly upset about this suggestion, stating that their daughter needed to grow up and act more independently. I suggested to them they would lose nothing (except a few more nights of sleep) if my suggestion didn't work.

They set the old crib up in their daughter's bedroom right next to the new big bed. The daughter was delighted to climb into the crib and slept through the night on the very first night the crib was up. The little girl continued to sleep in the crib, and a grateful phone call from the parents had the addendum that they were now worried that she would continue to sleep in that crib until she could no longer physically do so. I suggested that they respect the innate drive of every child to develop independence and continue to allow her to sleep in the crib at least for a short period of time yet.

In approximately a week and a half the parents called and stated that their daughter spontaneously came up to them and reported that they could now take the crib down; she wanted to sleep in her big bed. The parents participated with the child in taking the crib apart and restoring it in the attic. The child had no further sleep difficulty.

The act of independence often requires a temporary act of regression. If parents do not give permission to the child to regress temporarily or to ask for help, the child does not feel safe enough to extend his or her level of performance and independence.

Paradox #7: "A child must learn to say no in order to be able to say yes."

The meaning of this paradox is that by saying "no" we establish disengagement or boundaries. Without that capacity children do not feel safe enough to truly let another human being be emotionally close and influence their actions and thought process. It is important therefore for them to say "no" so that in the interpersonal reciprocal relationship pattern they can let people influence them without the feeling of being "taken over."

This particular paradox played out in the life of my granddaughter, Allison, when she was just three years old. It struck me one day when she was playing at our house that I had never heard her say the word *no*. When I asked her to say the word *no* she did so compliantly, albeit very weakly. I responded, "Grandpa wants you to say the 'no' really, really strong."

She again dutifully made several more attempts, but they still were not strong enough for me, so I resorted to additional body movement to emphasize the word. I told her to say the word *no* very loudly and while she was doing it to stomp one of her feet. The two of us practiced this with much glee until I was convinced that it was a piece of her repertoire. I then sent her home.

It could not have been fifteen minutes later when I received a phone call from my daughter, asking me what I had done to Allison. I played naive and asked her to explain what she was talking about. Allison reportedly came home, took off her coat, and threw it on the floor. Her mother said to her, "Allison, you know you are not supposed to throw your coat on the floor. Please pick it up and put it on the hook."

Allison looked at her mother and, while doing a great stomp with one foot, stated, "*No!*"

I was delighted; however, I spent the next twenty-five minutes explaining to my daughter the developmental process and how important it was for a child to feel as if she had the capacity to establish boundaries and to set up a "no" barrier when she needed it. I did say to my daughter that it was now *her* responsibility to help Allison discriminate when the "no" was appropriate and when the "no" was not appropriate. (I just love being a grandpa!)

There is actually a corresponding paradox to this that states "The more you can say no, the less you will miss out." In our busy world people attempt to do multiple tasks and are constantly busy because of the incapacity to say no. They never really make connections with other humans and therefore constantly miss out on relationships because of busyness. Being able to make the hard decision and to say "no" actually can keep a person from missing out on the important things in life.

Paradox #8: "To be truly close to someone, you must have good boundaries."

The human being is truly a unique creation. Humans desire to be connected and attached and included. On the other hand, humans also fear being taken over, swallowed up, or overshadowed by someone else. I view attachment on a continuum. On one end of the continuum is the totally unattached person, and at the other end of the continuum is what I term the hyper-attached person. On the hyper end of the continuum there are no boundaries, nothing to separate one person from another. It's as if symbiosis has taken over.

Both ends of the continuum represent fear to humans. At the unattached level there's a fear of loss of significant love objects. At the hyper-attached level there's a fear of loss of self. Mahler talked about it in terms of loss of individuation or loss of identity. When two people have good boundaries they know very clearly where they leave off and another person begins, and they respect the space between people; they have the freedom to be as close to someone else as they want to be. In order to be truly close to someone, it is critical to respect all the different kinds of boundaries they have, whether it be space boundaries, body boundaries, emotional feeling boundaries, or spiritual boundaries. When boundaries are respected and adhered to, the two humans are free to be close and as intimate as they want to be without the fear of loss of themselves.

The NCAST publication from the University of Washington lists sixty-five disengagement cues identified in infants, as opposed to nineteen engagement cues.[10] In other words, even from infancy children want to establish their own spatial and identity boundaries at the same time that they want to establish close, meaningful, intimate relationships. This is a continuous dance between one human and another: looking for closeness and a feeling of connectedness while at the same time respecting and feeling as if one is a separate individual.

Paradox #9: "The more you give yourself away, the bigger you become."

Mothers and teachers of preschoolers are constantly giving themselves away by nurturing and attending to young children with all of their beings. At the end of the day these nurturing people can feel very spent and tired emotionally. By giving themselves away they end up being "bigger" by virtue of the fact that the children integrate many parts of their characteristics and actions. Through the process of identification and introjection (an unconscious incorporation into one's own personality the characteristics of another person), the nurturing teacher finds pieces of himself or herself all over the classroom because of the positive nurturing influence. The same holds true with mothers who are nurturing their children and find that the characteristics that the children have are the result of identification. The larger the sphere of influence and the more you give yourself away within that sphere, the larger you become because of your positive influence.

Paradox #10: "To have someone on the inside is not to be trapped by that someone."

The "jealous lover" syndrome is described as one person wanting to know where the other person is constantly and obsessively. The jealous lover is actually trapped by his or her object of love because of the obsessive need to know where the love object is and what he or she is doing. The same holds true with small children who have not yet established solid representation, or pictures, of their significant loved people inside and therefore feel trapped by having to follow around the significant people and know where they are and what they are doing at every moment. If the significant love object is firmly implanted inside the other person in the form of memories and mental pictures, the child feels safe in knowing this significantly loved person will always be there.

A forty-year-old client came to therapy because she was constantly following her husband around, doing things with him and for him, and obsessed with where he was every minute. This lady was truly trapped by her husband in the sense that she could do nothing on her own unless her husband was with her or she knew exactly where he was and what he was doing. She even had to dress him and tie his shoes because of her need to serve him. She was angry over the fact that she was so subservient to him. While he attempted to take very good care of her also, he did his own things and could easily go places without including her.

This woman did not have him firmly attached and implanted on the inside of her mind and literally could not picture what her husband looked like if he wasn't in the vicinity. Her husband participated in the therapy process and helped his wife really get to know him and feel firmly attached to him so the feeling of fear that he would disappear or die started to subside. The therapy took a couple of years, but by the end this lady was able to help her husband out of her own choice and also established her own sense of identity apart from him. She no longer felt "trapped" by him, and the fear that he would suddenly die went completely away.

Paradox #11: "The basis of the capacity to be alone is the experience of being alone while some else is present."

It is impossible to learn to be alone by actually being utterly alone. The two-year-old may be playing in the living room of the family home while just around the corner in the kitchen Mother is preparing lunch or doing something out of sight from the two-year-old. The two-year-old is playing with some toys on the floor for a number of minutes and suddenly yells out, "Mom?"

Mother dutifully answers from the other room and says, "What, honey?" at which point the two-year-old says, "Nothing."

All the two-year-old wants to do is confirm that Mother's presence is in close proximity. Once the two-year-old is sure Mother can hear him or her and is close enough to be attentive, the two-year-old is content to be alone. Learning to be alone therefore is a process of knowing that there are significant love objects available for you and able to help you if they are needed. Practicing to be alone is practicing not to interact or ask for help when you know someone is absolutely available!

Sometimes my wife and I have ridden together in perfectly good moods for three hours without saying a word to each other. At our destination she would suddenly be aware of the fact that we had not talked for almost three hours and say, "It looks like we just practiced being alone." The human being is constantly practicing to be alone but can only do so with the full knowledge that a safe and helpful person is and will be available.

Some children will panic at being left alone because they were never allowed to be alone in the presence of a significant love object or safe person. They were never allowed to play by themselves and simply be watched and attended to by the significant adult. Learning to be alone, therefore, is learning to be in the presence of a significant person who loves and cares while at the same time not directly interacting with that person.

This paradox is also relevant for the student in school who does not seem to have the capacity to work or study alone. If a student does not feel safe because there are few significantly attached people that give the student that safe feeling, then the student constantly needs someone there in order to concentrate or work.

Paradox #12: "The less connected we feel, the more communication devices we invent."

This isn't exactly a child development paradox, but as a society we continue to become more dependent on technology: cell phones, pagers, personal digital assistants, faxes, web browsers with voice recognition. While all of these wonderful inventions are an attempt to connect people, in my practice I see that more and more people feel disconnected and unattached. Technology may be an attempt to compensate for, or at minimum keep up with,

an increasing number of people feeling unattached and disconnected. What all of the communication devices have accom-
plished is to give us an illusion that we are "connected" to another
human being.

This particular paradox may go back to the basis of the capacity
to be alone and people needing to practice being alone and knowing they may have someone on their cell phone at a moment's
notice. Technology is wonderful, but a cell phone call, even with
video capability, pales in comparison to actually sitting down, gazing
into another person's eyes, and holding a meaningful conversation.

CHAPTER 5

Object Constancy

The opposite of love is not hate, but rather nothing. The opposite of nothing is object constancy. Object constancy is an object or person planted inside of one's memory: a vivid, clear picture of a safe person. Mahler defines *mature object constancy* as "when a love object is not rejected or exchanged for another even if it can no longer provide satisfaction."[11] Mahler is saying that the safe person picture is on the inside so solidly that even after this person can no longer nurture, soothe, or protect, he or she is still a significant part of the life of the person. Fleming goes on to say that ideal object constancy is when "the emotional memory of the need satisfying object (mom or dad) can be evoked under the adverse conditions of increased need tension and frustration caused by delayed gratification or the person's absence." Once a safe person is planted on the inside of a child, even when that child is in stress and tension that person still holds a special spot in the child's mind.

So many adults today (and by adults I mean parents) have such tremendous emotional and physical needs of their own that they find it almost impossible to set them aside and give to their children. If the child has good ideal object constancy, then that child can feel his or her parents' presence even when there are periods of time when the parents cannot give to their child or when the child is angry at the parents and wants nothing to do with them. When a person has whole object constancy, which is like whole attachment (we can use those terms interchangeably), the significant loved person is now on the inside, and the child now wants to be able to do for himself or herself all the functions that the adult person did for the child. Good object constancy, or whole object constancy, really starts the child on the pathway of performing all of the functions that the adult has been expected to perform for the child in the childrearing process, so that the child is now maturing and starting to be able to take care of himself or herself.

Good object constancy is like having that caretaking person on the inside of our heads talking to us, as if that caretaker is standing right by us. We now, because of good object constancy, are able to soothe ourselves, reassure ourselves, guide ourselves, define our roles, identify who we are versus who another person is, appreciate our own skills and talents, nurture ourselves by taking care of ourselves, and hold ourselves, and we also protect ourselves by saying "no" and avoiding danger. The maturing child, because of object constancy, identifies with that adult object that is constant in the brain and is now performing all the functions that the outside person would do for the child.

The child development paradoxes that would go along with object constancy are letting someone go by putting him or her on the inside. (This would include school separations, significant moves, and even death.) Secondly, to have someone on the inside is to not be trapped by worry that the person is going to disappear. Thirdly, we learn to be alone with good object constancy because we have the person on the inside. And fourthly, the maturing child demands less attention when good object constancy is in place because the child has the voice and the picture on the inside that offers direction, safety, and protection. Without good object constancy the developing child would not be able to let people go, would worry all of the time, and would not be able to tolerate being alone or to function independently.

Object constancy is another huge building block in the developmental sequence of the growing child. There are techniques that will aid in the development of good object constancy. In discussing the development of object constancy, please keep in mind that this is not specifically a phenomenon that happens between an adult and a child. It can and should also happen between two adults, especially in a potentially loving relationship. For our discussions, however, I will focus upon the development of good object constancy as it pertains to the adult (parent) and the developing child.

The first way to develop object constancy is to establish a regular framework or a routine that is very predictable. In child development, consistency and regularity and predictability provide the kind of security for young children that helps them plant parents on the inside. Infants can assess that their environments, and particularly the caretaking people within their environments, are safe within ten days after being born. They can tell whether or not their environment is safe and responsive by how they are touched, whether or not people are predictable and constant, and the response time of their caregivers. A regular routine represents trust to the child, and it facilitates the internalization of the safe object or "love object." When children have a safe, constant love object caring for them, they tend to see other people as safe objects also, and they look at the world as a relatively safe and exciting place within which to grow.

A regular framework would include things like having the same people care for the child constantly and providing protective limits for the child that include the ability to say "no" and follow through with that. It means a brief but concise set of rules that young children should live by. (Simple rules for children should start when the child is about eighteen months of age. The ability to conceptualize rules and the brain's capacity to make sense of the meaning of these rules really does not start to develop until about eighteen months. Before that time it is virtually impossible for the child to understand rules.)

By eighteen to twenty-four months of age the child watches the parents for their personal congruence, which includes body language, verbal language, carry through or follow through, being on time, touching appropriately, and never lying. It is easy to lie to a young child by simply not telling the truth out of a perceived sense of protection. When Mommy has a splitting headache and the two-year-old asks, "What's wrong?" the mother, wanting to reassure the child, says, "Oh, nothing, honey. Everything is fine." By doing so, the mother is lying to the child, who knows full well that the mother is somehow not okay. It is much more congruent and safe for the child to hear the mother say she has a headache but she took an aspirin and everything will be okay in a little while.

In brain research, particularly that done by Bruce Perry,[12] it has been noted that personal congruence—regular consistent predictable frameworks—actually patterns the brain and contributes to brain development because it provides the feeling of safety. Eric Jensen, a noted educational and learning specialist, states that a disorderly environment conflicts with the brain's natural tendency to perceive our surroundings as an organized whole.[13] This actually affects how our brains perceive the environment and therefore can actually affect behavior because of our lack of trust.

The second technique to aid in developing good object constancy is for the adult to be a protective stimulus shield. Most young children between the ages of birth and twenty-four months receive excessive stimulation. The developing child actually needs protection from two sources of stimulation, namely external stimulation and internal stimulation. The external stimulation is most harmful if it is excessive between the ages of zero and eighteen months. The internal stimulation is something that children need protection from more between the ages of eighteen and thirty-six months.

A child born with no physical anomalies has at birth a normal stimulus barrier shield. This is the child's ability to tune out too much noise, too many people, too much light, etc., by simply closing his or her eyes, turning away, and going into what would be called a "rest cycle." The baby, however, needs additional stimulus protection and, especially in that first year of life, should be protected from overstimulation in terms of loud parties, being passed around at football games, or being subjected to a lot of jostling and bright or flashing lights. Please remember that developing object constancy parallels developing a relationship, and this is all about being protective and protected. While I would not advocate that a parent sit at home with the baby the first year of life, the majority of infants today receive excessive stimulation, which can be harmful to brain development and a feeling of safe interactional reciprocity.

Jane Healy, in her book *Endangered Minds: Why Children Don't Think and What We Can Do About It*, states that too much external stimuli temporarily puts the pleasure center of our brain out of commission, which literally stops a pleasurable interactional process between an adult and a child.[14] Adults should protect children from being excessively teased and purposely frustrated in order to see a "cute reaction."

The adult should also protect the child from internal stimuli. Slightly older children between eighteen and thirty-six months are constantly testing to see if they are safe and whether or not they will be structured or stopped if doing something dangerous and will even provoke the parent to see if they will be protected. A child's provocation is often an actual attempt to establish a safe object or to see if their love object will reject them, get excessively angry, or protect them. Children who often need protection from themselves are usually "shallow breathers," a technique children do to keep themselves hyper-alert.

It is not unusual also to see a counter phobic child (a child who is genuinely fearful but who overcompensates by looking fearless) taking dangerous risks. These risk-taking children need tremendous protection from themselves and in fact are begging for it. A serious parental mistake would be to allow a severely risk-taking two-and-half-year-old or three-year-old to take a risk as a way to "teach him a lesson." What in fact the parent would be teaching is that the environment is not safe because the significant love objects in the environment are not willing to step up and stop the child from doing something potentially dangerous.

Another way to protect the child from internal stimuli is to intervene and stop children from criticizing themselves when they can't do something or when they feel they've done something wrong. While it is good that children develop some healthy guilt and the ability to critically access what they are doing, excessive punitive verbalizing is unhealthy. Children oftentimes will be much harder on themselves than their parents are, so parents can help by interrupting the child's self-critique.

The third technique to develop good object constancy is to invest special time with the child. The best way to spell love is T-I-M-E. What parents do with their time is something that young children watch very carefully! Many parents take pride in giving each child equal time, but children are unique and special, and often one child will need more expenditure of actual time than another child. To be cared about uniquely for one's own special self is to be cared about as much as we need to be cared for. Every child will need individualized time and experience with the significant love object.

Investing special time with young children encompasses a number of specific points. One simple way to give the child special time is to make eye-to-eye contact while the child speaks. This type of "focused attention" (Dorothy Briggs) is something that nurtures the child at his or her very being. The parents' capacity to focus on the child and make eye contact is directly related to the student's attention span later in life during the school years.

A second way to invest time in a young child is to be the "perfect mirror."[15] Mirror the child's achievements by standing in awe of the child with facial expressions, body language, and what is said. As an example, if a three-year-old says, "Look at me" and then stands on one foot demonstrating his balance, your response is to open your mouth, be amazed, and state with huge surprise and pride on your face, "Look at you; you can balance on one foot!" That kind of mirroring of the child's achievement is an investment in motivation and self-pride. It is an investment that pays dividends for years to come in their developmental process.

A third way to invest time is to give the child permission to ask for help. Many young children believe they cannot or should not ask adults for help. Of course when a child asks for help, it certainly should be forthcoming. This kind of simple permission to "bother" the adult tells the child he or she has value and has permission to interrupt the adult world for a developmental question.

Another way to invest special time is to write your child encouragement cards. If, after a family gathering, you realize that your four-year-old behaved particularly well, after everyone has left or possibly even the next morning sit down and write a small card to the child, stating that you appreciate how the child listened, helped, or interacted at the family get-together. If the child is too young to read, write the card and then read it to the child and watch that child keep the card as a reminder. Every time the child sees that card, the good feelings of appropriate behavior will stand out in the child's mind. This form of appreciation and describing the child's behavior is something that is a powerful intrinsic motivator for the child. The child places these words on the inside and uses them for internal motivation, particularly during days when it is a struggle to maintain appropriate behavior.

Another way to spend special time with children is to touch them often. Hugs, pats on the back, high-fives, handshakes—any form of appropriate touch is an investment in the child and is relating to the child that he or she is special. It is interesting to note that the English word *neglect* actually comes from a Latin word *neglere*, which literally translated means "not to touch." Sometimes all children need is for a significant adult to place a hand on their shoulder. That simple investment is enough to produce the kind of motivation the child needs at that particular moment.

Another way to spend special time with the child is to just "stand there." When I was growing up my father would often say to me, "Phillip, don't just stand there; do something." He was attempting to motivate me to see work that needed to be done without having him point it out. However, it is equally important for adults to simply be with the child in order for the child to feel special.

There are children who, particularly in the early elementary grades, do not seem to be able to complete their homework assignments unless a parent is sitting with them, watching them and being attentive. These children perform for the parent when the parent simply stands by and watches in an approving and awestruck manner. By simple virtue of the parent's presence, the child seems more capable of performing than if left alone in a room to complete the assignment.

Attentive silence also teaches the capacity to be alone. Parents need to learn that when we are too busy doing things *for* our children, we forget how important it is to simply *be* with them.

Here are three additional ways to spend time with children. First, turn off the television set. This is a powerful message to the child that conversation between the parent and the child is more important than a movie on TV. Secondly, eat meals together. The act of sitting down around a table gives the child a twofold feeling of nurturance emotionally and physically. And finally, never ever again buy a Hallmark card. In our family we make our own cards and put in these cards our own thoughts and feelings in the form of the card's verse. The entire greeting card industry is built upon the premise that we do not know how to express our feelings in words. If you buy a card at all, it should be blank inside. Practice writing your own feelings and expressions of love using your own words. These cards are some of the most precious cards that I own, and there is a giant box under the master bedroom bed that contains well over thirty years of precious expressions both from my children and from my spouse. The children have also kept many of those cards that my wife and I have written to them, and this becomes a source of continual affirmation of the love and connection and the good object constancy within us.

The fourth technique to aid in developing object constancy is for parents to encourage the utilization of transitional objects. A transitional object soothes a person by evoking a feeling of safety. The most common transitional object is a child's "binky," the little rubber pacifier that gives a nonnutritive soothing to the young child simply by the child performing the sucking motion. Most people need "binkies." Particularly in early childhood, however, the developmental sequence in its most abbreviated form goes like this: The young child first holds the real object, in other words Mom or Dad, in order to be soothed and to feel safe. As children develop they hold transitional objects, which actually stand for and remind them of the real object. Finally, as children mature they put that soothing human object on the inside of their heads in the form of a consistent mental representation, and now they are able to hold and soothe themselves. The utilization of transitional objects therefore is an assist in developing good constancy, made up of clear mental pictures.

Anything that represents a soothing and safe feeling to the young child can be considered a transitional object. This could be a special blanket, hand lotion rubbed on the child's hand, a picture of Mom or Dad or someone safe, or the parent's keys or glove.

When my wife traveled to Florida from our home in Michigan to see her parents one winter, I took her to the airport on a cold and snowy day. She was wearing a big down-filled parka, which she left in the car because she obviously would not need it when she landed in Florida. She asked that I bring the parka when I picked her up a week later. When she returned she was pleasantly surprised that I remembered to take the parka along. I accepted her appreciation but did not tell her that the parka rode next to me all week. Yes, it was the efficient way to remember the parka, but I am willing to admit that my wife's parka offered me a transitional object. It was soothing to get in my car each morning and see that parka sitting on the passenger side and even be able to smell my wife's cologne. Transitional objects come in many forms and in fact offer most individuals a feeling of security and reassurance.

In my therapeutic practice I often require parents to institute transitional objects with their children and also require parents to carry pictures of their children to show the children that they are symbolically always being held. In this technologically advanced age the new "binky" is today's cell phone, the constant reminder that we are "connected" or can be connected to another person. It is also a sad commentary in my opinion that the more disconnected we feel, the more communication devices we invent.

The fifth technique to develop object constancy is to encourage reality testing: encouraging children to ask questions and giving them factual answers. To a small child the greatest fear is of the unknown. When parents help children test their reality by answering factually and talking in concrete, open language, children start to construct real images of the world around them.

Reality testing is also helpful when a child says, "I can't." Ask that child if he or she heard a voice on the inside saying that he or she couldn't or if the child heard someone on the outside say that he or she couldn't. In this way, children differentiate the voices that they hear on the inside that they have taken in from the actual voices on the outside that are speaking to them. This is good reality testing to know what we think versus what may be heard on the outside.

Young children have many feelings, and parents should attempt to validate those feelings, which then facilitates children's belief in themselves and their own perceptions. Children must be able to validate what they feel as real feelings and then be able to differentiate whether or not their feelings have any justifiable rationale within the environment. It is important to validate the feeling first before testing out whether or not the feeling is in fact valid in the external environment.

Also encourage children to recognize their own boundaries, such as body boundaries, possessions boundaries, and verbal boundaries. Recognizing personal boundaries keeps us feeling safe and often on good terms with other people.

In the process of helping children test out their reality it may be necessary to discount a primitive thought process that I call the "law of repetition." Most young children believe that if anything has happened in the past it can and will continue to happen in the future. This is not necessarily good reality testing, because past performance does not lock in future happenings within the environment.

If a child's parent should die from cancer, the young child automatically believes that the other parent will die, and then the child will die, and all of the child's other relatives will die. Encourage the child to see and test out the reality using the information provided from the adult mind. If the child has a trust in the adult, the child is able to more readily adopt the reality testing of another person and feel safe that the "law of repetition" really does not hold up in many circumstances.

Encourage reality testing when it comes to cue reading: identification of nonverbal messages such as facial expressions, tone of voice, and body language. Young children often quickly perceive another person as being an aggressor when in fact there was no aggression involved. If the adult is not there to help children read cues, these children can grow up to be poor cue readers and subsequently take things personally and react violently to things inappropriately. This is especially true of the learning disabled child or the child who has a sensory integration dysfunction. Good reality testing when it comes to cue reading keeps the child from perceiving that other people are always out to mock him or her. When we promote good reality testing we are promoting the picture of good objects on the inside of our child's head.

The sixth technique to encourage object constancy is to help the child develop mental images. By eighteen months the child should have the ability to start placing a vivid mental picture of a significant love object on the inside in the form of a visual picture as well as an emotional sense of security. To help the process of mental imaging, encourage children to draw pictures of their families and also of the significant events within their families. Parents should set up frequent rendezvous with their children so that the child has practice time to hold the parents in mind. If your child asks you to read a story, arrange for the child to select a book and to meet you on the living room couch when the big hand reaches the number twelve. The time should only be about four or five minutes away so that the child doesn't have long to wait but does have to hold a picture of you reading a story before the actual event. Setting up frequent rendezvous is a way to develop a good consistent picture or object on the inside of a child's mind. It is also a way to establish trust.

Additional techniques to develop mental representations would be to encourage the child in role-playing, developing skits, and using all kinds of imagination. Drawing pictures and telling stories about the pictures is also a good way to set object constancy in place. Ask young children who they talk like, who they walk like, and who they act like in order to get them to picture significant love objects within their environment. When children memorize proper names of their friends or teachers, the names themselves can conjure up mental representations of the people. It is also a good idea to put children's pictures around the house and also cut out pictures from magazines that represent the occupations that children aspire to. This way, children not only have a mental picture of who they are now, but they also can develop and form a mental picture of who they will become in the future.

It is also important for parents to hold good pictures of who their children can become in their heads. The greatest intrinsic motivator comes from perceived abilities and perceived competence. In other words, if parents perceive their child as developing into something or someone worthwhile, that is a powerful motivator and a powerful mental image that their child will inevitably strive for, even if it is unspoken. A four-year-old once told me, "When somebody loves you, you know they love you just by the way they say your name. When they say your name you can see that they are thinking good about you."

The seventh technique to develop good object constancy is to be empathic with the child. Empathy is the ability to perceive and feel what another person feels. Empathy in its simplest form is the ability to be silent on the inside and listen. (The word *listen* contains the exact same letters as the word *silent.*)

I once had an eleven-year-old patient who developed what we coined "Muppet Therapy," which was nothing more than being empathic and reflective. The name came from the two old geezers of Jim Henson's *The Muppet Show* television program. When Miss Piggy gave a stage show there were two old geezers in the balcony who would critique the stage show. The first old geezer would start out saying that it was the most awful show that he had ever seen and that everyone was out of step and he wondered why anyone would ever want to watch a show like that. The second old geezer would then say that yes, it was a terrible show, and most everything went wrong, but there was one thing that he really liked. The first old geezer picked up on that one positive thing and then mentioned there was one other positive thing in the terrible show that he liked, and this continued back and forth until the two old geezers who had started out trashing the stage show were now praising it as one of the best shows they had ever seen.

This eleven-year-old stated that if parents were more like those two old geezers and would simply listen and be empathetic with their children and then drop in maybe one small positive, the children would pick up on the positive and the empathy. By doing this, the parent could help direct the child toward a more positive outlook. This eleven-year-old, in teaching me "Muppet Therapy," was able to cure himself and also help train his own parents in the process.

It can really demonstrate empathy when a parent verbally walks through a problem-solving process with the child. An example of this might be asking the child four questions after he smacks his brother with a Tonka truck. The first question is "What did you do?" This gets the reality out. Secondly, "When you did that, what did you want?" Thirdly, "List four other things you could have done other than smack your brother with the truck." And finally, "What will you do the next time?" After this is done, a logical consequence to the child's behavior can be implemented; however, the empathic training process will not be forgotten.

Seeing alternatives via an empathic process is a huge self-esteem builder. The children who have the poorest self-esteem are children who cannot see alternatives, and if one road is blocked they simply sit in a heap, unable to move.

The eighth technique to assist in development of object constancy is to teach children to accept and tolerate ambivalent feelings: having two different feelings at the same time toward one object. It is important for young children to be able to develop simultaneous conflicting feelings toward one person and to be able to tolerate those feelings. Children after the age of eighteen to twenty-four months should be able to love their mommy dearly and be angry with her at the same time and to realize that the relationship is not lost because of the conflicting feelings. The way to teach this is to state to the child that it is possible to be angry with Mommy or Daddy but still love Mommy or Daddy too.

The child may retort, "No, I don't love you when I hate you."

The parent should respond, "When you get a little older you'll be able to understand that you can feel two different things at the same time toward one person." If a child does not develop this capacity he or she will never be able to establish consistent friends or even a good consistent mental picture of a safe love object. When a parent helps a child tolerate ambivalent feelings, it really helps the child feel safe on the inside, because the child knows that feelings are not always loving and kind and can be both positive and negative toward a person at the same time.

The ninth technique to facilitate the development of object constancy is simply a reminder that we are human. I ran across an article in my readings many years ago that referred to the "70 percent rule," which states that at most a parent can only attend to a child 70 percent of the waking time. Parents need to give themselves a break in terms of whether their focused attention is enough. If we look in detail at this 70 percent rule in an eight-hour day, which is 480 minutes, a normal human being can only attend and completely focus on a child 336 minutes, which is 70 percent. That means that for 144 minutes, which is equivalent to two-and-a-half hours out of every eight hours, it is not possible to focus on the child. Adults also have to have rest cycles and to briefly disengage from the child.

It is helpful, however, to tell the child when we would like a few minutes to think, to write, to talk on the phone, or to do whatever is restful. This does not mean isolating yourself from the child, and of course a young child should always be within proximity or view of the parent. Telling the child that this is what the parent needs is being really respectful to the child as well as being respectful to the parent's own emotional and psychological needs. When parents are that respectful to the child and to themselves, it develops an accurate picture of the consistent love object on the inside rather then the fantasized all-perfect and all-attention-giving person that no one can really be.

It is important for parents to model what I term "anger metabolism." The word *metabolize* simply means to break something down to its basic component parts. When adults metabolize their anger, they break down their anger into the component parts of hurt and fear and are able to label these to their children. Anger metabolism in my opinion is a physical and emotional process continuously going on in living organisms by which anger is broken down into hurt or fear or physical energy and made useful for vital functioning in maintaining relationships.

Anger often frightens children. This includes the anger of parents as well as the child's own anger. It is not unusual for me to hear children as young as three years old refer to their anger as a "dragon on the inside" or a "monster" that sometimes gets loose. This tells me that children are afraid of not only other people's anger but also their own monsters within. When parents can model anger metabolism to their children, this makes the expression of intense feelings safe enough for children to mentally represent that parent in a realistic yet safe manner on the inside of their heads.

There is a three-step anger metabolism process that could be helpful to parents and also soothing to the child. The first step would be for the parent to label the feeling of anger and break it down verbally into its components of fear and hurt or other emotions. When the parent labels the feeling, the child is able to see that the feeling is not totally out of control, and the child also realizes the focus of the anger, which may or may not be his or her behavior.

The parent then redefines anger as "practice." We all get angry, and by practicing anger appropriately we are practicing to feel safe and in control. Anger is also used to correct a relationship closeness between people and can be used to establish boundaries between two people.

Thirdly, the parent can model ways to sublimate anger: to channel anger into appropriate expressions, such as physical activity, exercising, walking, drawing, writing a note, or calling up a friend. Children often construct a play or a skit and act out anger in a safe medium using make-believe. When parents model appropriate anger they become learning mentors for the child and someone who is okay to incorporate as a safe picture on the inside. Young children will have in their bank of mental pictures either mentors who are safe or monsters who are not safe.

It is also my opinion that all children need a mental file or a "Rolodex" of people on the inside they can pull out at a moment's notice to feel safe and feel connected and to feel real. When children have safe pictures and consistent objects on the inside, they truly are free. The child is then free to play, free to experience joy and pain, free to learn, free to explore, free to take some calculated risks, and free to grow.

CHAPTER 6

Empathy and Self-Esteem

This chapter is about the development of self-esteem, but because empathy is such a valuable component of self-esteem, I also want to look at the development of empathy in detail.

In the book entitled *Your Child's Self-Esteem,* Dorothy Briggs relates what she calls seven active ingredients to communicate love and build self-esteem.[16] I have seen evidence of those seven ingredients as I have treated young children.

The first ingredient is *focused attention.* Focused attention is more than listening: it is an all-present being with someone. When I sit in the family room with the remote in my hand, my wife knows enough to walk over to me, take the remote from my hand, and turn off the television in order to talk to me. She realizes that I will not be "fully there" unless I have no distractions, even though I may answer her questions and hold a conversation with her. A focused attention is complete with both body and mind paying attention. That sense of inner presence as well as outer presence feeds the young child's self-image and self-esteem like nothing else can.

Focused attention is most needed when a child is under stress. When a child goes to preschool for the first time or a new baby arrives or the family moves to a different location or a different house, a child experiencing any kind of loss will need tremendous amounts of true focused attention. This ingredient then builds self-esteem and a sense of value within the child.

The second ingredient is to *develop trust* with the child. Margaret Mahler's developmental sequence also includes basic trust as a fundamental ingredient for the child's sense of self-esteem. One of the child's first concerns is for personal safety. The building of trust can happen in many ways but mainly by telling the child the absolute simple truth.

When a three-year-old asks a parent where he or she is going and the parent simply says to the store, neglecting to tell the child that they are also stopping at the pediatrician's office for a booster shot, that parent undermines the sense of basic trust with that child. Whenever a child is prepared for future events such as doctor visits, the child will be able to feel as if his or her environment is predictable and trustworthy.

It is impossible to hide significant events or feelings from the very young child. It is always better to very briefly, very simply, keep the child informed as to what will happen, when, and to whom. Parents do not need to tell the child all of the facts and may certainly withhold details; however, to maintain that sense of trust and to build trust, honesty is the best policy.

The third of Briggs' ingredients is *being nonjudgmental.* Rather than saying to the child "You're mean," it would be more appropriate to say "I do not like hitting to get what you want, and you have to stop it now." It is difficult for parents to switch from being a judgmental, label-making person to a reacting, describing person. Dr. Haim Ginott, in his book *Teacher and Child,* talks about "perils of praise."[17] He asks, "Is praise constructive or destructive?" Most parents believe that all praise is constructive, but that is not the case. Even praise can be judgmental.

I went to a kindergarten classroom to observe a child who was having behavioral problems, and while I was observing the class, the teacher had to step out and told the children that anyone who needed help was to ask the gentleman in the back of the room (me). Knowing that such a daunting task was a little like trying to herd cats, I sat quietly in the back of the room, hoping for the best. To my great relief, the kindergarteners walked around the classroom talking gently to each other, continued to work on their individual projects, and were really quite marvelous during the absence of the teacher.

When the teacher came back and saw how well behaved her classroom was, she stated in a loud voice to all of her class that she was so pleased that she had "such a wonderful classroom of little angels." Immediately three fights broke out, the class turned to chaos, and it took a good twenty minutes before the class felt safe and under control again.

Later the teacher asked me what I thought happened when she walked back into the classroom. I was fairly sure that because she had judged her children, even though it was a positive judgment, it created tremendous anxiety in the children to be called "angels." Most of the children knew full well they were not angels. It was quite evident that even praise can be destructive rather than constructive if done in a judgmental manner.

Dr. Ginott talks about appreciative praise, which is completely nonjudgmental and describes for the child what has taken place and how much the observer appreciates it. If the teacher had walked back into the classroom and stated to her class, "Oh children, my eyes say thank you so much for working hard while I was gone," the teacher would not have had any problems upon her return.

The other major thing that judgmental praise does that is destructive to the child's sense of self-image and esteem is that it does not allow children to assess themselves accurately on the inside. When a child is labeled either *good* or *bad*, the child no longer has anything to say. However, to appreciate something that the child has done and to express that appreciation allows the child the opportunity to say "I'm good; I did a good job." The child needs the capacity and the freedom to be able to talk to himself or herself on the inside and label internally rather than be labeled externally. This is where self-esteem and true intrinsic motivation come from.

The fourth ingredient that Briggs lists is *being cherished*. The word *cherish* is not in use much today. It is defined as to hold dear and treat affectionately. This is both externally and physically as well as on the inside, to keep fondly and hold dearly in mind. To cherish a child is to hold that child on the outside as well as on the inside. Prizing children as the true miracles that they are and investing in children, not as an extension of one's self but as truly living, breathing human beings, is to fully cherish. The acid test for whether a child is cherished is to ask "Do I habitually notice something missing?"

When raising our own children I had a daughter who struggled with math concepts while in elementary school. If she would bring home a math paper that had sixteen math questions on it and two of them were wrong, I tended to focus on the two wrong rather than the fourteen right. It is difficult for parents to really see what's right and what's not missing and to value their child, particularly if they themselves were not valued as children. Self-esteem develops best when we see children as the true miracles *apart from ourselves* they are.

The fifth ingredient is *allowing children to own their own feelings.* At a local supermarket, a three-year-old sat in a cart as the mother hurriedly unpacked the groceries onto the checkout lane. The child whined, "I want candy, Mommy. I'm hungry." The mother's response was, "No, you don't want candy, and no, you're not hungry!" Letting children own their own feelings does not mean letting children do anything they want. When we talk about ownership of feelings we are talking about the freedom to feel, not a total freedom to act. It is absolutely essential for children from a very young age to get their feelings validated.

In a book entitled *Liberated Parents, Liberated Children* by Adele Faber and Elaine Mazlish,[18] this point is driven home. The book tells of an eleven-year-old girl who was at a local swimming pool when an older boy asked her if he could lick her toes. The girl ran home and told her mother that she felt "funny" about what the boy said. The story demonstrated that when children validate their own feelings, even if it's a vague perception such as feeling "funny," they in fact could be saving themselves a great deal of pain or even their lives. A child's trust in his or her feelings and perceptions can literally keep that child safe!

If, however, we deny a child his or her perceptions, we tend to dull the ability of that child to sense danger and by doing that make the child vulnerable to the influences of those who may not have his or her welfare at heart. Owning and validating feelings is certainly an important ingredient, not only for safety, but also to a sense of a child's self-esteem.

The sixth of Briggs' ingredients is *respect for uniqueness.* In order to help the child develop self-esteem, the adult has to remember that growth is not in a straight line. The child often takes two steps forward in maturation and one step backwards. Regressions are completely normal in the developmental process and unique to each individual child. If a child is given the option to retreat *without dishonor,* this makes the child much more likely to embrace the unknown, try new things, and become successful.

Uniqueness and the respect for uniqueness therefore mean making it safe for each individual child to take small risks and even experience failure. When a reporter asked Thomas Edison, "So, Mr. Edison, how does it feel to have 1,400 failures in your attempt to perfect this light bulb?" Edison said, "Young man, I have not failed; I simply found 10, 000 ways that do not work." The unique aspect of every child's pattern of growth is something that, if respected by significant adults, creates a sense of real self-esteem.

The last ingredient that Dorothy Briggs lists is the *development of empathy.* Empathy is an understanding that is based in the love for another person and understanding that person's point of view. Empathy in a relationship between a parent and a child goes a long way to reducing and neutralizing the child's aggressive tendencies.

The development of empathy seems to be on a continuum (see figure 2). Empathic responses are behaviors learned from the young child's caregivers. During the first eighteen months the child is unable to identify feelings and is only initially starting to connect feeling responses to specific actions in the real world. The parent therefore takes over the empathic function for the child and actually attempts to feel for the child. If a child should fall and Mommy says, "Oh baby, that hurt, that hurt," Mother is really defining for the child the feeling and in some respect feeling for the child.

In the next stage, the child has a greater perception of self as a separate individual and, by the age of two, is able to name the outside world and begin to name feelings on the inside. Mother and child form a mutual admiration society, and the mother still represents a consistent presence and a source of comfort. Now when the child gets hurt, the mother realizes that the child can label his or her own feelings, although the mother very much feels with the child.

A mother might say, "Oh that hurt, didn't it?" This indicates to the child a real sense that the mother knows what the child is feeling and allows the mother to label it but still partake in some of the pain.

A child of five years of age has complete cognitive processing, has the ability to abstract, and has a good knowledge of how the family functions and the type of care available from the parent. The child by this time is able to "see" the parent on the inside in the form of a mental picture or representation. When the child is hurt the child can literally see the parent go into a soothing, comforting function, and the child feels in touch with that parent even though the parent may not show up immediately when the child is hurt. Friends are included in the child's repertoire of soothing and comforting people, along with a system of rules regarding how to soothe based upon the nurturing process given by the caregivers. The child now has an internal "knowledge" of the other people in the environment who are capable of doing soothing tasks, and the child who has been nurtured kindly will feel in touch with the soothing loved one internally. This makes the child capable of soothing himself or herself at least for a period of time until external soothing agents actually arrive on the scene.

By the time children are approximately nine years of age the major portion, if not all, of the ability to regulate themselves has been internalized, and children function fairly autonomously. They soothe themselves by changing their physical state (standing up if they fall down, sitting down if they bump their heads, or rubbing their heads or making other physical soothing movements) and are able to be their own "good mother." If the child has progressed to the ability to not only empathize with other human beings but also empathize with himself or herself, the child has reached the maximum point on the empathic continuum scale.

A young adult has reached the maximum growth benefit of the empathic continuum scale when he or she has the capacity to say "no." Without the capacity to say "no" this person cannot fully take care of himself or herself and protect himself or herself within the environment. There is a paradox involved in this process that states "The more you can say no, the less you will miss out." We as people cannot take in and do everything within our environments, and therefore we need to pick and choose what kind of activities we are going to be involved in so that we are not scattered in our functioning. People who attempt to do all things actually miss out on everything. It is a secure feeling to be able to realize that one has reached the end of the empathic continuum development and is now able to fully care for self as well as others.

When caregivers do not assist young children in the developmental process along the empathic continuum, there are progressive pathological symptoms that occur. If a nurturing caregiver is not available to feel for the child in the first eighteen months, the child will be seen as protesting in the form of physical behaviors such as rigid muscles, sleeplessness, fussy eating, exaggerated startle response, ticks and grimaces and hiccups, gagging responses, and general tension reactions.

If the lack of nurturing responses continues into toddlerhood, what I often see is the child trying to self-soothe with self-stimulation because there is no presence of a "safe other." The child may go into head banging responses or sucking nonnutritive objects or rocking back and forth on a continual basis.

Children unfortunate enough to continue to be left to their own devices as they get into the school-age years may "numb out" when they've been hurt and blank out any injuries or situations where the empathy of others would have been soothing. A consistent pattern of non-empathic caregiving can lead to depression in the young child and often a lethargic apathy or even self-destructive action.

Experiencing empathic resonance is vital to the acquisition of a sense of self and a sense of self-esteem. Self-esteem starts at birth within an environment that tells the infant he or she is safe and will be well fed and taken care of. It is then that the child starts to believe that he or she has worth, and this belief is carried into adulthood. At every point in the development sequence, valuing the child will produce a person with high self-esteem who cares about, and empathizes with, others and is capable of taking care of himself or herself.

Figure 2

Empathic Continuum

0–18 Months	18 Months–5 Years	5–8 Years	9 Years and Up
Merge with idealized parent Names the "outer" world "Other" seen as functions of self Parent consistently responds and is soothing EMPATHY = available caretaking	Separateness of bodies Admiration— awe EMPATHY = "presence," a source of comfort	Friends and family available during stress Mental representation EMPATHY = "knowledge" of the "other"	Initiative— self-soothing Locomotion Ability to proactively regulate own self-esteem (See alternatives) EMPATHY = "action" (Self-empathy— we are our own parent)
FEEL FOR THEM	**FEEL WITH THEM**	**FEEL INTERNALLY IN TOUCH**	**FEEL SECURE**

Developmental Progression When Child Ignored

Protest No caretaking	Self-stimulation No presence of "safe other" Rocking Head banging Sucking objects	Blanking out Numbing out Not knowing is better	Depression Inaction or self-destructive action

CHAPTER 7

Preschool Thought Process and Trauma Regression

It is now time to take a look at early thought process as it pertains to the developing child. In my work with children, I have observed that the primitive thought process will reappear in older children when they are under extreme pressure or have gone through trauma. As we discuss some of the developing primitive thought process, I will explain how older children and even adults regress in their thought process back to this early primary thought in order to feel safe and in control.

I will cover eight different types of thought as if we were looking through the eyes of a three-year-old. The three-year-old thought process is liberally sprinkled with primitive (sometimes called primary) thought, and it is important for adults to understand and be able to see the "logic" in very young children's perceptions.

The first thought process has to do with egocentrism. The egocentric child obviously thinks egocentrically. The word ego stands for "self"; *centric* means the center. Therefore the child believes he or she is the center of the universe. When the two-year-old child starts to realize that the parents are no longer placing the child at the center of the universe, the two-year-old will act out. A normal two-year-old temper tantrum is born out of indignation that the big people no longer will allow the world to revolve around the child.

This egocentrism is quite normal for the young developing child but looks on the surface as if the child is extremely selfish. When parents tell me that they have the most selfish two-year-old in the world, I simply state, "That's what a two-year-old is all about."

The two-year-old is just learning that reality and big people are going to dictate what's going to happen in his or her environment.

When young children feel and perceive egocentrically, there are a number of implications for the child. Time is irrelevant to the egocentric child, which makes sequencing events difficult. *Today, yesterday*, and *tomorrow* are difficult concepts, as young children tend to live in the moment.

Another implication of egocentrism is the child's limited ability to empathize with others. A two-year-old is just beginning to feel for himself or herself and therefore has a difficult time empathizing with anyone else. A three-year-old can hit another child with a stick and then wonder why that child cries. A full and complete capacity for empathy is not totally in place until about the age of nine years.

Another implication for egocentrism is that young children do not understand a whole picture. It's difficult to make sense of complete acts with motivation and consequences, which is why abused children believe they are abused because they themselves are bad. It is very difficult to perceive others as bad and to make sense of complete situations. Childhood egocentrism consistently says to the young child that whatever happened must be the child's fault, because the world revolves around the child. It also accounts for the fact that young children believe that parents should know everything that happens to the child, even if the child does not tell the parents.

An older child who has been traumatized may pick up the egocentrism again as a way of wishing to control his or her universe. Picking egocentrism back up may skew many of the cognitive processing functions, such as abstract thinking, problem solving, and even speech and language. Some adults who have had poor attachment and traumatic upbringing never really get rid of egocentrism and the thought process that goes with it; however, as they get into adulthood we no longer think of them as egocentric but narcissistic.

A second thought process in early childhood has to do with concrete thinking. The very young child is developing the ability to put things together, and it starts out as a one-to-one relationship. In other words, there is only one solution to one problem, and that solution is simple. In math, the concrete thinker would say that A plus B equals AB, not C, which would be abstract thought. If a young concrete thinker does not like his sister, he simply says, "Let's get rid of her." If the child wants a new bike, he simply would say, "Let's go to the store and get it." The younger the child, the more primitive the solution and thought process.

When I interact with children I want to assess whether their thought process is still mainly concrete. To do this I tell jokes. Concrete thinking children do not think concrete jokes are funny. When I say to a concrete thinker, "Why did the chicken cross the road?" and then answer, "To get to the other side," the concrete thinker simply looks at me like this is concretely logical, so why would this be funny? Or I might say to a child, "Which side of a dog has the most hair?" If the child is into abstract thought process they may say that they usually pet the dog on one side more than the other and therefore the side they do not rub a lot may have the most hair. However, a concrete thinker would answer, "The outside." My all-time favorite joke is to ask a young child where generals keep their armies. When I tell them the answer is "up their sleevies," the concrete thinker doesn't get it, because playing with words such as *arm* and *armies* completely eludes the concrete thinker.

The implication for concrete thinking children is to watch carefully what is said and what kind of abstract language, slang, or euphemism that is used. With euphemisms—words or phrases that stand for something else—children often gather different kinds of meaning. When I see a severely traumatized early elementary child (around the age of eight), I talk very concretely, trying to stay away from abstract slang or euphemistic language. Trauma tends to regress the mental ability to understand abstract language or completely comprehend all of the nuances in the English language.

A third process that young children utilize has to do with their translation of what others say to them in a literal manner. If an adult said to a literal translating child that he was fired at work, the child would picture that person on fire. When Daddy tells a child to keep his or her eye on the ball, the child looks quizzically at the father and says, "I can't do that."

The Amelia Bedelia children's books are an excellent example of literal translation. Children love to read these stories about an adult cleaning lady who translates everything that is said to her literally. When Amelia Bedelia is asked to draw the curtains, she takes out a piece of paper and draws them on the paper. These books are great fun for children who have advanced to abstract thinking because they recognize how silly Amelia Bedelia is, being an adult and still thinking in a literal process.

It is interesting to note that the lower the cognitive stage in the ability to process words, the more easily children seem to be traumatized. If a parent unthinkingly says to a very young child, "I'm going to break your neck," that child literally translates that and becomes terrified. It is quite easy for adults to inadvertently set children up for subjective feelings of helplessness, simply because young children think differently and process in a literal manner. Again, a traumatized older child does tend to fall back on literal translation for a sense of control, and any child who has sustained a trauma will need concrete training in reading cues and interpreting the euphemistic English language.

Two experiences from my practice involved very young children traumatized unwittingly by well-meaning adults. A three-year-old was going to preschool a couple of days a week. He came home from school one day in tears, stating over and over again to his mother that he liked his name. The mother said that she liked his name too; in fact, she was the one who had named him. She wondered why he was so upset. The child, after being soothed, was able to say to his mother that his teacher told the children that at Christmastime they were all going to exchange names. This was an abstract concept that blew right by this child and actually caused distress.

Another incident was a young child who was brought to me because he was not sleeping. Through play I was able to ascertain that this child, who had a piece of hair standing up toward the middle of his head in a pronounced cowlick, was terrified because his father told him the reason he had a cowlick was because when he was sleeping at night a Jersey cow would enter his room and slick his head. The child then became terrified that there were giant cows loose in his room at night and refused to go into deep sleep.

The father was mortified when he found out and was able to reassure the child that what he said was "make-believe" and that he would never let any cows into the house and especially into his bedroom. (A quick note: asking children questions while reading a book with them improves their capacity for developing abstract thought and the many meanings of words.)

A fourth thought process of the young child is called a self-referent understanding level. These are children who want to know why but do not have the abstract ability to use any reference point other than themselves. Things will makes sense only if they have had a similar experience.

When my niece was three years old my sister was pregnant with her second child. My sister gained a great deal of weight, and, being the traditional sweet brother that I am, I would tease her about being "as big as a barrel." One day my niece said, "Uncle Phil, I know how the baby gets out." She sat down and started to explain that when "it's time," Mommy goes to the hospital. I nodded in agreement, and she went on to state that the doctors take her to the "operation room." Again I nod my head in affirmation. Then she stated, "All the doctors and people gather around Mommy and screw her head off. Then one doctor reaches down inside of Mommy where it is all yucky and pulls the baby out. Then the doctors pick up Mommy's head and screws the head back on."

I'm sure my eyes were as large as saucers. I stated to her that the head part was not really true, but I should have known better than to argue with a three-year-old, because she was adamant that her version was absolutely correct. So...how did this three-year-old come up with this story?

On my sister's kitchen counter was a big glass barrel filled with pickles. It had a screw top to it, and whenever a family member wanted a pickle, he or she would screw the top off, reach in, and pull the pickle out. And it was tradition in our family to call the little children "pickles." My niece took what she knew self-referently and rather exquisitely extrapolated that to the birthing process.

When one knows the details of the child's environment and remembers that children think very self-referently, it is usually an easy step to figure out the thought process. The implication for adults in terms of this understanding level is that one needs to learn the child's frame of reference. One also needs to know the environmental situation and happenings that occurred in the child's life. Because of that self-referent position, children who are traumatized believe that everyone else is also traumatized and knows exactly what the trauma is and why they are acting out. They also believe if they're upset or crabby, other people must be too. They will also assume if they were hurt by adults, then all adults are unsafe. This thought process often shows up in severely traumatized children who start to generalize and believe that all people and all objects in the world have become dangerous.

A fifth early process has to do with an active fantasy life. For most two-, three-, and four-year-olds, nothing is too farfetched. I recall the movie entitled *Mr. Mom* and how the little children in the family referred to the vacuum cleaner as "Jaws." Jaws would suck up anything in its path, almost as if it was a ravenous shark. I have seen young children pretend that people are like computers and should have interchangeable parts. One little boy stated that when his nose was stuffed up he wanted to unplug his nose and plug in a new nose, but he didn't know which store to get new noses from.

Most children use fantasy to feel a sense of control or to soothe themselves by creating their own scenarios. Active fantasies allow children to master their environment. It is not unusual to have a fantasy friend that is either human or animal. My niece had a fantasy giant pet gorilla that lived under the refrigerator. These types of fantasies are normal and are an expression of the child's ability to make sense of and analyze his or her environment.

Children also use fantasy to repair in their own minds traumatic events. Lenore Terr, a noted child psychiatrist, referred to the revision of the truth into fantasy as "recapitulation and revision."[19] I was in a preschool classroom when a three-and-a-half-year-old boy came running up to the teacher to tell her that the night before his mother's boyfriend started slapping his mother and even gave her a bloody lip. He told his teacher that when he saw that happen he came out of his room and yelled at the boyfriend, and when he paid no attention, he "kicked his butt."

The teacher was aghast at the intensity and the detail of the story. She looked at me quizzically, and I motioned for her to accept the story as it was. Later I explained to the teacher that this was a classic example of what Terr calls recapitulation and revision. It was an attempt on the little boy's part to master a traumatic event by use of his powerful fantasy. The teacher did report the event to protective services, but I asked the teacher to be attentive to the child in terms of the stories that he would subsequently tell her.

Sure enough, the next day the little boy said to the teacher that he really did not kick his mother's boyfriend's butt but did yell at him from behind the couch. The day after that, the little boy said that he was really too scared to come out of his own room and was hiding under the covers when this incident occurred.

The intensity of traumatic experiences puts children in such a helpless state that they use the fantasy to repair the event and see themselves as powerful and capable of assisting a loved one or getting themselves out of trouble. It is appropriate not to challenge the initial repairing fantasies of children and to accept the revision and the continual recapitulation of the event. This was a classic example of why young children need to act tough and spin these kinds of fantasies as a way to master fear and the tremendous feeling of vulnerability.

Ultimately the unvarnished truth does seem to come out of these children's mouths, but only after enough time has passed for them to realize that they are now safe and that the horror of the events can be talked about truthfully. To push children too rapidly in uncovering these kinds of traumas is inappropriate and disrespectful of the coping and defense mechanisms that help them to feel powerful and intact. In the young child an active fantasy life can be used for a multitude of reasons, and unless a child stays in the fantasy for the majority of the time, the fantasy process is therapeutic.

A sixth thought process in the young child is what I call the law of repetition. For the child, if something (anything) happened once, it can and probably will happen again. If the parent is late picking up the child from the babysitter, the child automatically starts to believe that the parent is going to be late every day. This means that a young child whose parent is diagnosed with cancer can easily believe, based on the law of repetition, that the other parent will contract cancer or the child will contract cancer and everyone will die. Accidents, abuse situations, catastrophic events, almost anything can be subject in a child's mind to the law of repetition. Because they believe so firmly, many children will push limits in their environment to see if it will happen again.

A young boy was brought to me for therapy because three months earlier he had been struck by a car after dashing out into the road after a ball. He had broken both legs, and after a three-month recovery period both legs were as good as new. Now, however, the mother had a difficult time keeping the child from dashing purposely out into the road. It was as if the child was playing "chicken" with the cars to see whether or not he was going to be hit and injured severely again. Children will push the danger envelope like this in a convoluted way to actually feel safe. They want the feeling that they have control over their environment and that the tragedy or the trauma will not happen again.

Another implication in dealing with this law of repetition is that children can believe that if they talk about something that was traumatic, it will then be caused to happen again. In addition, for the young child, witnessing a traumatic event is as traumatizing as being the recipient or the victim of a trauma event. Therefore the law of repetition applies not only to experiencing something but also to witnessing it.

The way to handle children who get wrapped up in the law of repetition is to question and to gently confront or challenge the child's thoughts. Reassure and soothe the child while pointing out that not every event repeats. Bring the child out of the fantasy of the law of repetition and into the reality of an environment that is now safe and protective.

A seventh preschool thought process is called *personification*. The word *personification* contains two words, the first being *person* and the second *fication*, which means making or production. So the word means a person production: a thing or quality or animal represented as a person, like Mickey Mouse. Young children often personify things that they do not understand or that frighten them.

I once had a little girl about the age of four in treatment who was terrified of going outside. It seems her beloved dog wandered into the woods behind their house and did not come back for three days. It was alive but barely, and there were cuts, bruises, and scratches all over the dog. The parents surmised that the dog wandered into the woods and cornered an animal such as a raccoon and ended up on the bad end of that fight.

For the little girl, however, the "woods" hurt her dog, and the woods became the personification of a malevolent monster. Every place she saw a small woods would become another monster in her eyes, until finally anything out of doors was monstrous and she became housebound. As she got a little older and was told the truth about what happened to the dog and how the woods itself had nothing to do with it, she started to see how she attributed lifelike qualities to inanimate objects. The fear gradually subsided, although to this day this person does not hang around any wooded area.

The process of personification can happen on a smaller scale, as demonstrated by a three-year-old who was watching a brightly colored pheasant feather as it lay on the kitchen table. A gentle breeze blowing through the sliding glass door lifted the feather approximately three inches off the table, where it floated for a second, and then it fell back down. The little boy started screaming, "It's alive! It's alive!" He ran to his bedroom and locked himself in. His eight-year-old sister, who was subject to a more rational perspective, thought this was hilarious and picked up the feather and headed toward the boy's room, exclaiming loudly, "It's coming to get you!"

This process of personification also incorporates a "splitting" process in that the child often splits off a dangerous part and personifies that part. When I asked a young child whether the man who allegedly beat him had hurt him, he stated, "No, but his big ugly fist did." The child split off a portion of the man, who was human, and personified the fist, which he then made into a separate human-like entity through the process of personification. Children will often do this to prevent having bad or hateful feelings toward a whole person.

It usually takes a fairly extreme trauma in order for a child to enter this process. It is my opinion that children do this because they do not want a major portion of their world to be unsafe, so they split the unsafe portions off where they can compartmentalize them and feel like it's not such a big scary intrusion into their world.

The process of personification can be therapeutic, particularly for young children. However, the process can be carried to an extreme if a significant portion of the world becomes personified and therefore dangerous. Lots of soothing, lots of reality testing, and a great deal of patience with these young children is needed, along with a little maturation so that the cognitive processing can become more reality oriented.

The last process of young children's thought has to do with a process of delayed reaction. It is not unusual for a child to suffer a fairly extreme trauma and show absolutely no symptoms or residual effects from that trauma for a significant period of time. It's almost as if the child says either consciously or unconsciously, "I will think of something else, because the traumatic event is too intense right now."

One vivid example stands out in my mind of a young boy about the age of eight whose family suffered a horrific automobile accident. The father and daughter were killed instantly in the accident, and the mother and this little boy were seriously hurt, although their injuries were not life threatening. The little boy recovered quickly and within two weeks was back in school. The teacher saw no symptoms of depression, the child's grades and his study habits were excellent, and his social interactions did not seem to be affected one bit.

Meanwhile, his mother was recuperating and was going through a serious depression, as any person would after losing one's spouse and a daughter. The mother's injuries were healed after about six months, but her severe depression lasted almost eighteen months. All through this time the little boy functioned normally, almost as if nothing had happened to their family.

At the point when the mother was coming out of her depression, the boy absolutely fell apart. His grades plummeted, his social interactions became aggressive and alienated, and he started losing weight. The teachers and school counselors wondered what was going on and did not tie it to the accident, which happened over a year and a half before, because of this youngster's fine performance in the interim.

When I started to see this child in therapy I found that he had completely put on hold his mourning process for his father and sister. He also had tremendous anxiety about the welfare of his mother. At one point in the therapy process he stated that he could not express or feel anything because he did not have a person there to support him with these intense emotions. He knew that his mother was unavailable because of her own depression, and it was not until the mother became available emotionally that this youngster almost literally said, "It's my turn." At that point he went into severe depression of his own, went into his mourning process, and worked through all of the anxiety and the emotion that had been stored up for over a year and a half.

It was amazing to think that the young child had the capacity to completely compartmentalize and put on hold everything that was welling up within him until it was safe in the environment to actually go to work on it. I have had many such cases and am now a huge believer in this process of delayed reaction. (I am also a huge believer in a critical incident stress debriefing process, whether or not a child or adult shows symptoms after the trauma.) The implication of this is that even if the child denies it or shows no symptomatic behavior, it is imperative to move in with lots of supports, to encourage the child to talk, and to make the child's environment completely physically safe and emotionally supportive.

There are many more thought processes that young children are involved in; however, this chapter has outlined enough of these processes for the reader to gain an appreciation of how differently young children think and the capacity of all older people to go back to primitive thought processes under stress or trauma.

CHAPTER 8

Boundaries and Contagious Emotion

A vital but often overlooked function in the early child development process is the establishment of boundaries. In today's world, boundaries between people are constantly being blurred, and the emotions that are expressed are so scattered that it is difficult for a person to differentiate what is being felt from what has been put upon the person. Parents and adults give lip service to the concept of boundaries and how contagious emotions really are but do not practice the establishment of good boundaries. Without good boundaries the contagion factor of intense emotions between people becomes uncontrollable.

Boundaries are behavioral limits. Boundaries are separating lines between one person and another person that establish individual identity and thought process as well as physical separateness. Boundaries are limits that protect the space between parent and child as well as between two adults.

When it comes to the establishment of boundaries between two human beings, it is actually quite a skill to stay in a "zone of helpfulness." As a parent it is a skill to refrain from being under-involved or detached or unempathic with the child and at the same time not to be over-involved or enmeshed or merged with the child. Under-involvement and over-involvement are both perceived by children as the parents not liking them. Children see under-involvement as a loss of attachment with the parent, and they see over-involvement as a loss of their own sense of identity and separateness and who they are. Anything outside of the zone of helpfulness is perceived by the child as a loss.

I have taken a bit of flack in my career for preaching the concept of boundaries. The flack usually consists of being accused of being cold, aloof, insensitive, or possibly stoic, Victorian, or platonic. I believe firmly, however, that good boundaries make good relationships.

Boundary Types

There are a number of boundary types, the most obvious being physical boundaries. This has to do with touching and physical contact, such as hugging, kissing, patting, handshaking, etc. Physical boundaries even between a parent and a child are essential because, while I advocate that parents touch children as much as appropriately possible, touching can also become intrusive and a boundary violation. This includes a well-meaning dad who tickles his child way past the point of the child enjoying the interaction and makes the child cry because the tickling game has become too intense.

Another boundary type is emotional boundaries. This refers to emotional states. My emotions do not necessarily match your emotions; neither do they have to. I will talk about emotional boundaries a little later when discussing the contagious emotion factor.

There are also spiritual boundaries, in that what I believe may be different from what you believe. Children generally embrace their parents' beliefs, but they may also have mentors who are so important in their lives that a different kind of belief system may be embraced.

There is also a mental boundary, in that people do not think alike, and it is important for parents especially to respect the thought process of the child. It is also helpful to understand the different ways of thinking that children have at different developmental levels.

There is also a verbal boundary. This particular boundary I find very interesting in that it is constantly being violated, both by parents and by children. Listening when someone is talking has become a lost art, and interrupting conversations seems to be, in many families, a way of life.

It is a verbal boundary violation for parents to answer a telephone when they are discussing something with their child. It could also be a verbal boundary violation for the child to use offensive language. Verbal boundary violations are prevalent in today's world, and that disrupts a significant portion of our capacity to relate in a meaningful fashion with one another.

There is also a personal space boundary. Space boundary represents the distance around a person that is personal space. A forty-year-old lady came for her first appointment time and sat down in the client chair, approximately eight feet from me. This woman slid the chair forward, until her knees were literally touching my knees, and then started to talk with me. I was extremely uneasy with this and considered it a boundary violation.

Because my chair is on wheels, rolling on a large plastic mat under my desk, I moved my chair backward a couple of feet. To my surprise, the lady scooted her chair up to the point where her knees were again touching my knees, and she continued to talk.

I thought to myself that I would give her one more nonverbal cue, and I backed up another foot and a half on my plastic runner, only to find her moving up against my knees again. At that point I rather loudly said, "*Stop!*" I even made a stopping hand gesture and stated that she needed to back up because she was violating my personal space.

The lady looked at me rather aghast and then looked down at the large plastic runner on the floor on which I had my chair. She said, "I'll make a deal with you. Everything on that plastic runner is yours, and the rest of the floor space can be mine." She moved off the runner, and I moved to the middle of the runner, and we began in earnest the therapeutic session. This put her approximately four to five feet away from me, and we established what I felt was a much more comfortable spatial boundary.

Approximately four sessions later this lady asked me if I recalled the first session, when I established spatial boundaries. She reported she had gone to four other therapists within the metropolitan area, and not one of those therapists asked her to back away and was willing to hold the therapeutic session in a close proximity. She said, "People who do not have boundaries are not safe people." She said she could not be close to anyone or even trust anyone until she knew for sure that they had firmly intact boundaries. This was dramatic confirmation of how important boundaries are in any relationship.

There is also a skill boundary. Parent and teachers who go beyond their skill levels, or training and experience level, without seeking assistance or help are asking for trouble. It is important to recognize the limits of our skills and not violate our own skill boundaries.

There's also a time boundary. Parents need to have time away from their children and have a real personal boundary around when they can spend time with adults away from the demanding emotional time with children.

The last boundary is what I call "stuff" boundaries. *My stuff* and *your stuff* really refer to personal belongings. Materials sitting on my desk are not to be touched by young children; neither are my personal desk drawers play areas for young children. Children should have their own spaces, their own drawers, and their own closet space.

Respecting space and the "stuff" within space is a needed lesson in boundaries. It is inappropriate for parents to give away or throw away "stuff" that belongs to their children without their children's knowledge and permission. This may take some persuasion at times, but the trust built between the parent and the child is well worth it.

Another example is a parent who wants to move the child's bedroom. It is inappropriate to move the child's stuff while he or she is out and have the child come home to a house where all of the "stuff" is relocated. This represents a boundary violation that can result in mistrust that will last for years.

What Good Boundaries Do

If boundaries are respected and kept consistently, a number of good things happen within the family. First, the trust factor within the family is solid, and the child always believes what the parent says. It also promotes honesty and truthfulness within the child, because the child can depend upon people within the child's environment.

Good boundaries also help keep the child as the focus of interaction, because when boundaries are violated mistrust, anger, and suspicion invade personal relationships. Boundaries also help to set up good relationships faster and promote truly close interaction because there is little danger in being violated with respect to boundaries.

Good boundaries also develop frustration tolerance. When children can't touch other people's things or must ask and request permission, this increases the child's ability to tolerate frustration and to wait. It also corrects the fantasy that all things belong to the child and are free game to use or destroy at will. Once children realize that the boundaries will be established and enforced, they lose many of their fears that revolve around loss of objects or loss of people or loss of their own identities.

Good boundaries also encourage more sophisticated coping skills, such as verbalization, rationalization, and sublimation. Sublimation is rechanneling energy into another activity. People with good boundaries, particularly adults with good boundaries, offer the young child a positive identification figure who is safe, trusting, and fun to be with. Parents really have no chance of teaching boundaries if they themselves do not keep boundaries.

What Poor Boundaries Do

The consequences of poor boundaries within a household give everyone in that household excessive stress. Without boundaries it's almost impossible to know who has ownership of problems and feelings, because those emotional boundaries are not defined. Poor boundaries also promote dependency and mistrust, which then generalizes to all people, even outside of the family.

An adolescent client, describing his parents, said, "I love my parents for what they did for me; I hate them for what they did to me." They were involved in all of his activities in a non-boundaried way and ran interference for him at all times. They bought him what he wanted, when he wanted it. They bailed him out of jail and completely backed him in all of his activities, including immoral, illegal, and intrusive actions. The parents thought they were standing up for their child, but they were not requiring that the child have any kind of boundaries established within his life. This led to a young man who was constantly in trouble and ended up giving much sorrow and grief to both parents and himself.

Another consequence of poor boundary enforcement is that once the adult starts to violate boundaries, a slippery slope begins. More and more boundaries become violated, and oftentimes the end result is a child who does not know what role he or she fills. Small boundary violations lead to larger and more excessive boundary violations, until finally it's difficult to determine roles, ownership, or even identity.

Recall an old fable on how to boil a frog. One can never boil a frog by throwing a frog in a hot pan of boiling water; the frog will simply leap out. If, however, you put the frog in cold water in a pan and then put the pan on the burner and slowly heat the water, the frog will be cooked before it realizes what has transpired. The same is true with boundary violations. One boundary violation leads to another violation and another, until finally the parent and the child are cooked.

Another consequence of poorly enforce boundaries is that parents start feeling used. Allowing children to violate their boundaries, use their space, or not ask for permission eventually becomes a source of frustration to parents. Parents start feeling taken advantage of by the child when in fact they have allowed the child to violate the house rules and boundaries.

Common Signs of Boundary Violations

One of the common signs of boundary violations is excessive verbalizing without listening. In parenthood this often betrays the parents' anxiety over a given topic or the need to be right or in control.

Another sign of boundary violation is quickly yielding to the child's request. This violates the child's potential to do things solo and use problem-solving skills.

Inappropriate physical contact could also be a boundary violation, especially when the child asks the parent to stop.

Breaches of confidentiality can also be boundary violations. If the child asks the parents not to divulge what was told to them but then the parents tell the grandparents everything, that is a boundary violation and a breach of confidentiality that leads to a significant loss of trust.

Parents who can't say "no" also are frequent boundary violators and are probably allowing children to violate boundaries as well.

Parents who share adult and personal topics with a child are also violating boundaries. It is inappropriate to relate to a child intimate sex-life details. Parents who dress inappropriately, in an extremely provocative manner, also violate boundaries and embarrass their children.

Something that parents do not often think about is that they are violating boundaries by giving the child unrealistic praise. Sometimes well-meaning parents will praise their children excessively for minute or even questionable success to the point of coming off fake to the child. This unrealistic praise and encouragement is actually a boundary violation representing a violation of truth. Children are not helped by unrealistic encouragement or praise and generally can see through that as a potential manipulative technique on the parents' part.

There are many more potential boundary violations, but the point is that boundaries are essential in establishing safety and healthy relationships between children and adults. The most loving and healthy adults are adults who help children establish good boundaries and maintain good boundaries for themselves.

Contagious Emotion

Parents and teachers often ask how young children or even middle-school-aged children have the capacity to evoke so many feelings in the adult. Emotions are extremely contagious, and unless we are aware of our own boundaries, other people's emotions often invade our feelings, and we find ourselves feeling with, or even for, other people.

As children get older they are able to own their own feelings, but at a young age the essence of what is helpful for the child lies in the process of the adult making himself or herself available to receive the child's projected feelings. The adult then feels these feelings and utilizes his or her mature personality by digesting or metabolizing these feelings and figuring out an appropriate reaction or behavior that will deal with the feelings that have been passed along. By doing this, the adult really is teaching the child what I call "affect modulation."

Affect modulation means the child needs to be able to tone down the intensity of his or her feelings, and by giving them to other people, particularly adults, the child is taught through behavior how to handle intense feelings. This takes time and some interaction between the adult and the child. It is not a bad thing for young children to pass their feelings on to adults in an effort to learn how to handle those feelings and thus mature in a way so that stress and intense feelings do not become overwhelming.

In talking about contagious emotions, I need to define two psychological terms, the first being *projection*. Projection is a cognitive and emotional process whereby the child attempts to completely get rid of a negative feeling or action or thought. The child does so to maintain his or her own self-esteem, avoid criticism or punishment, or just kick the bad feeling to the outside, where it's much easier to combat. It is much easier to fight an opponent such as an impulse on the outside than attempting to control the impulse on the inside. This is one reason why young children often criticize themselves after the fact even though they could not have stopped the behavior before it happened.

A two-year-old child may pick up Mommy's expensive vase (knowing full well she was told many times not to touch the vase) and bring it to Mommy and state, "No, no, don't touch." The child is criticizing herself after the fact, but it is easier now to get a grip on the impulse to touch the vase by actually bringing the impulse to the outside, bringing the vase to Mommy, and demonstrating to her an attempt to grasp the concept of self-control.

Projection can be so strong that the person who is doing the projection feels completely separate from what is being projected. In other words, projection is a strong form of denial. The projector does not necessarily want the person being projected upon to feel anything; the sole purpose of projection is to get rid of something.

When my son was about four years of age he loved to play with the garden hose and would do something that annoyed both his mother and me by digging holes in our lawn with the power of the water stream. Whenever we heard the water hose go on, one of us would run outside to see if our son was digging more holes. On one occasion I found him standing as if he were completely oblivious to the fact that the hose was running full blast at his feet. I asked the parental question "Were you playing with the hose?"

My son said that Johnnie, our neighbor boy, was playing with the hose; however, Johnnie was nowhere to be seen. In fact, I pointed out that the neighbors were gone, but our son had projected the bad action onto someone else. This projective action was to get rid of the responsibility for this behavior and to escape possible punishment.

The other term that needs defining is *projective identification.* In this psychological process the projector, usually the child, wants to get rid of a feeling, but only temporarily. The child does not want to disown that feeling completely but wants someone else to feel it and to see how that person handles it. If it's handled well the child will identify with the good handling behavior and take back the feeling. It is an attempt to live with oneself without completely getting rid of all of the aspects of that particular piece of the self.

The official definition of *projective identification* is the ridding of the self of unwanted aspects of the self, such as helplessness, fear, rage, feeling stupid, etc., and depositing those unwanted parts or feelings onto another person and then, depending on how those feelings are handled by that other person, recovering them in a digested or metabolized version.

Unfortunately, when we get feelings projected upon us, the adult's tendency is to become anxious and attempt to not feel the projected feelings and to ward off intense emotions without trying to understand them. Think of children as being tuning forks. If you hold two tuning forks together and strike one of them and bring it within ten inches of the silent tuning fork, the silent tuning fork will start to vibrate at the same decibel level. Each child vibrates at a certain decibel level, and when he or she gets around other people, whether children or adults, the child's level of vibration often will bring the vibration level in the other person to the exact same point.

It is imperative that parents, because of their love and attachment, allow children to pass on their intense immature emotions and help them to deal with tension and stress. In today's world, we see many children who panic quickly, get stressed out at a moment's notice, and simply do not know how to handle intense emotion. Not enough parents are willing to be "used" in this process and help children to feel and analyze their emotions.

It should be noted, in light of the previous discussion on boundaries, that parents need to consciously allow themselves to feel some of these feelings so that they can differentiate the boundaries between their own feelings and the child's.

There are a number of reasons why children use the psychological process of projective identification. The first reason is defensive. It actually gives the child distance from intense emotions like rage. When children can put these intense feelings onto an actor outside of themselves and watch what that person does, they reassure themselves that people do survive even when the feelings are extremely intense.

Children often personify things, and they often personify feelings. It is not unusual for children to say that if they feel all of the anger they are feeling inside, it will literally kill them. They personify the anger as a vicious adversary or internal monster rather than an intense emotion that is capable of being handled.

Some children use projective identification as a form of communication. When children project their feelings onto an adult, that adult knows exactly how that child feels even though that child cannot put it into words.

In my office I was working with a very angry eight-year-old boy and his mother. The mother also brought her infant son to the appointment, and she allowed the baby to crawl around on the floor in front of the eight-year-old boy. The boy was having a difficult time explaining to me what he was feeling. Suddenly, the eight-year-old stomped upon the baby's fingers, and the baby let out a scream of pain. The mother jumped up, and I must confess that I felt rage within me at this deliberate act. I stopped myself from reacting and looked at the eight-year-old, who was looking intently at me! I then realized that the eight-year-old had completely projected onto me the intensity of his own rage.

I was now feeling the rage full force. I looked at him and said, "Now I understand." With that, the eight-year-old burst into tears and was able to continue a very emotional session regarding how hurt and angry he felt. I am certainly not advocating stepping on babies' fingers, but the event gave me the opportunity to tell the child he was understood and that I read and felt his communication fully. It also gave me time to let the eight-year-old boy know that his raging emotion could be controlled, because I controlled my emotions.

Children also use projective identification as a form of connecting and relating. When another person feels your emotion and you know that they feel it, there is a one-to-one connection with that person. Children want to be able to test out their perceptions by using an adult's ego strength to deal with the emotion. It is a plea for help to feel connected with someone who has a stronger ego capacity and impulse control system. In some ways it is an exquisite mechanism on the child's part to force the adult to share the adult ego. (Adults have to have been loved enough as children to allow their egos to be shared without the fear of being emotionally used up.)

The final reason children use projective identification is to find pathways to change. If feelings are processed by another (emotionally stronger) person and made available to the child for reinternalization, then that child can really adjust his or her personality and learn how to handle intense emotions. It is a great way for children to learn affect (feeling) regulation.

When parents feel helpless with a child, it's usually exactly what the child wants and needs the parent to feel. Parents should then ask themselves, Is this how the child is feeling? When parents are not invested in their own child, the process of projective identification can be disastrous. The parent may take those feelings and then act them out against the child, at which point no learning occurs and a vicious battle can rage.

Adults also use projective identification; however, it is not one of the more mature coping skills or defense mechanisms. Returning home from work in a particularly foul mood, I drove into the garage really fast and slammed on the brakes. I got out of the car and walked to the back door of the house, only to find it locked. It ticked me off even more to have to dig for my keys to get into my own house.

I thrust open the door and tripped on my wife's shoes. This ticked me off even more, so I kicked the shoes all the way down the hallway, grumbling as they sailed. Then I heard the washing machine "walking" around the utility room with an unbalanced load. I screamed at my wife for not even being able to balance a washing machine load. I then walked into the kitchen and noticed that there was no supper cooking on the stove. I then screamed at my wife for not having supper ready when I got home.

At that point my wife appeared from the living room red-faced and screamed back, "Fine! Now I'm angry! Are you happy?"

I was, in fact, now very happy, because I was now feeling calm. I had completely projected my angry emotions onto my wife, and she certainly took them and felt them intensely. Of course I did pay a price for behaving in such a manner, but this is an example of how adults use projective identification to unload their own emotions. (And please note: this example was a rare occurrence with the precious wife I have been blessed to share life with for the past forty years!)

The internal process of projective identification progresses in four steps. The first step involves the fantasy of projecting a piece of yourself (i.e., an emotion) onto or into another person. When children say to me "I have a dragon inside of me," they usually mean they are afraid of their own raging possibilities and reaction. They then enjoy the fantasy of taking that dragon and planting the dragon into someone else to see what will happen and whether that dragon is capable of being mastered. These children are emotionally contagious people and often have profoundly blurred boundaries. These children expect others to feel the same way they do and, in fact, are hoping that they will learn from this situation.

The second internal piece of this process has to do with getting the adult (the object of the projection) to accept the projected feelings. The child then has to pressure the adult to think and feel and act in a manner that is congruent with the projection. Just because children are "dumping" their feelings does not mean that they are not willing to learn from the projection by identifying with safe and appropriate responses.

Children use a number of pressure methods to get others to feel what they feel, the first being to ignore the parents and treat the parents as if they don't exist. This is usually powerful for parents who "need" their children to love them or acknowledge them as nurturing people.

A second pressure method is actual physical intimidation, such as the time a therapist friend of mine was in the home of a single mother whose boyfriend was not pleased that this therapist was visiting. The boyfriend brought a chainsaw into the living room, where the mother and the therapist were talking, and started the chainsaw up. He revved the engine a couple of times, at which point the therapist said her good-byes to the mother and left immediately. When she told me the story, I congratulated her for the correct response but then noted that the boyfriend had completely given his anxiety over to *her* and now she was feeling all of the fear and perceived danger of a home visit.

Other pressure methods include hyperactivity and hyper-vigilance. Some children create anxiety in adults because of their pinball-like motion and their excessive physical activity. Other children who are a little older can "yes but" parents and get parents to feel completely helpless. Parents can say to their child, "Have you tried this or that?" and the child responds, "Yes, but it doesn't work." The child continues to say "yes but, yes but" until finally the parent is completely worn out and feeling helpless.

At that point, it behooves the parents to recognize the helplessness that is being projected onto them and to reflect that back to the child. The parent could say, "I am feeling so helpless right now because I have given you every idea I could think of and you are telling me that nothing works." By hearing that the adult understands the feeling of helplessness, the child now becomes empowered to look more closely at some of the remedies and make them his or her own.

Other kinds of pressure include verbal threats to hurt self or others. It's best not to take these threats lightly; however, this is often a projection to get the parent to feel the pain and the fear that the child is feeling. These pressure methods work best with people who have somewhat blurred boundaries. Hopefully as adults become better at picking up these projections, when the blood pressure goes up the parents ask themselves, "What is it that the child is trying to tell me?"

The third phase of projective identification is the taking in of the projection by the adult recipient and breaking it down into its component parts. It is the job of the parents to process the thoughts, feelings, and behavior options that are open to them when the child makes the projection. The parent should first of all contain the feeling and allow himself or herself to feel it for a brief moment. The parent should then label the feeling that the child is unable to articulate, whether it is helplessness, fear, rage, humiliation, rejection, aloneness, confusion, etc. After labeling, the parent quickly and cognitively analyzes how the child got her or him to feel those emotions.

Adults should recognize a real danger here when emotions get projected upon them. Adults may get flashbacks from their own past but must avoid responding to them. As I sat in a preschool classroom watching a table of children during lunchtime, one particularly angry child picked up his bottle of milk, looked straight at the teacher, and purposely poured it out onto the table.

The teacher got the projection of rage and retorted back to the child, "Do you know who you remind me of? You remind me of my ex-husband; that's why he's my ex." The point to this example is that projected emotions often link up with our own past, and adults have to be careful not to allow that to move us to premature action. We should only do a silent interpretation of our own "stuff" and stay with the child's emotion and what the child is trying to tell us.

The final phase of projective identification is allowing the projecting child to take back his or her emotions. Once these emotions have been put into words (labeled) by the parent and validated, the parent starts a cognitive problem-solving process out loud with the child. What has the child done before? What has worked? What could be done now to solve one piece of the problem? If the parent does all of the steps, then the child inevitability will accept the feelings back, because the child can see that no one is consumed, no one is hurt, no one goes crazy, and people are capable of handling the emotions in an appropriate manner. It is so comforting to the child to see that feelings can actually be mastered.

This also is the process whereby children learn not to panic in situations. This reassurance of shared emotion with a parent figure is one of the best ways to raise a child who can regulate feelings and see the world as a challenge rather than a threat.

There are uses of projective identification for teachers also. It is a way to educate each other and ourselves on how to handle other people's emotions. It also teaches awareness of what we feel because it evokes our past by the present emotions. It also tests our ability to contain our own anxiety, at least temporarily, which is an important modeling process.

Becoming good at handling projective identification also causes us to be more team oriented with other adults, because often it is essential to share our feelings and to support each other so that when intense emotions arise we can work them out rather than act them out. It is my hope that from now on the people who have read this chapter will be asking, "Does this emotion come from me, and if not, what am I being asked to help them with?"

CHAPTER 9

Kindergarten Competence

A well-nurtured, securely attached youngster is the best prepared child for learning and school performance. This child will probably have mastered all the competencies necessary to thrive in school.

I've identified sixteen areas of competencies kindergarteners should have learned by the time they enter kindergarten. This list represents the important issues for not only their cognitive processing but also their emotional life.

1. Children should feel good and safe about trying new experiences. Children should be unafraid to use all of their senses—sight, smell, hearing, touch, and taste—to try out different things. They should be willing to look at cause-and-effect relationships, such as a tadpole turning into a frog or a seed developing into a plant, and love to wonder about these things.

Children should also feel comfortable with letters and numbers. They should have fun doing geometry, which is nothing more than putting pieces into the puzzle and making a whole picture. Letters should be fun for them, and grouping letters into something that means their name should be an exciting activity.

2. Children should know what their special strengths and skills are. Some children have a gift for memorizing, some have a gift for coordination, and some even have a gift for categorizing. Each child should know what he or she is especially good at and revel in all of his or her strengths, and especially "special" strength.

3. Children should enter kindergarten happy with their identity: their sexual identity, role identity, and emotional identity. They should be happy to be a boy or to be a girl because they heard their parents say, "I'm so happy you are my little girl [or boy]!" They should be happy to be a son or a daughter and fit into that role. They should also be happy to be emotionally attached and connected to significant brothers or sisters or parents. They should also be happy about belonging to an ethnic group, whether African-American, Hispanic, or Polish. It is important for young children to feel that they belong, not only within a family, but also in larger social groups.

4. Children should have achieved independence *and* interdependence. By kindergarten age children should feed themselves, dress themselves, go potty by themselves, brush their own teeth, pour their own milk, and generally problem solve on a daily basis.

They also need to have achieved a certain amount of ability to self-soothe when they're scared, when they're lonely, or when they're angry. When they're scared they can hold something that belongs to a safe person and use it as a transitional object. When they're lonely they can express that and ask for closeness from the people around them. When they're angry they need to have various soothing mechanisms or simple behaviors that reduce their emotional intensity and calm them down.

These children should also be able to tolerate separations and, because they have had trusting people within their past environment, be able to trust new people within the school environment. In other words, these children will need to have the capacity to say "hello" to new people as well as to be able to say "good-bye" to their well-attached people.

5. Children should have self-control. Children need to come into kindergarten with the ability to accept external ego lending, which is learning to borrow patience and strength from another person if their own patience runs out. They need to know that it is okay to ask for help and also to make decisions. These children need to be able to observe themselves and get feedback from their peers and adults around them to help them judge whether or not their behavior is appropriate within a group setting.

These children need to have the ability to wait, at least for a short period of time, and well-attached children have the capacity to do that as a result of promises that have been kept. The whole process of handling anger and frustration is something that should be mastered to a significant degree, even though we know that every child will get angry at some time. The skill is in how the anger is expressed. Children also need to know that anger is used both to put distance between people and to draw people closer and be more protective.

6. Children should be comfortable in the use of verbalization. Expressing wants and needs is also a vehicle to self-control. To be able to articulate is to possess a certain amount of power.

As I was observing kindergarten children at play, one five-year-old gathered all of his buddies together in a circle, and I heard him tell them that he could, with just one word, make all of the teachers within the room come running over to him. His buddies were impressed but skeptical. The little boy asked all of his buddies to back up and, in his loudest and most desperate voice, yelled out the word "*Potty!*" Sure enough, all of the teachers came running over to assist him in going to the bathroom. As he was being led away by a gaggle of teachers he glanced back over his shoulder at his peers, who were impressed that one word had such power.

The use of words is very important in the formation of mental representations (pictures) in children's minds. By using words they can practice doing things through their mental representation before they actually do them. When the mind practices in pictures, it helps to formulate a memory of successful actions before the actual event. This process cuts down on behavior problems and results in a feeling of mastery on the child's part.

7. Children need to know the pleasure of playing as well as the reality of sharing. It is said that adults laugh approximately fifteen times during a normal day and that young children laugh approximately four hundred times in the course of a normal day. The pleasure of playing is really a child's work in learning how the environment operates.

Sharing also is something that children cannot do until they have a feeling of ownership in *what* they have and *who* they have around them to protect their possessions and boundaries.

8. Children need to know their own emotions and be able to tolerate conflicting emotions. It is important for young children to have the ability to label what it is they are feeling and whom they are feeling this toward. They also need the ability to feel two different emotions toward one person at the same time. If children do not master this during the early ages, they will continue to work on this through their grade school years and even into high school.

It is essential to be able to tolerate conflicting emotions in preschool and to have mastered this by the time the child is in kindergarten. We learn to tolerate conflicting emotions when we are loved so much that we know we can love and be angry with a person at the same time.

9. Children need to understand rules. Children need to see the necessity for safety and organization, and that requires rules and procedures. They need to know that the reason we have rules is not to be mean or restricting but to keep children safe, which is a word that five-year-olds can relate to. Children need to know that rules are their friends, not monsters to make life miserable.

10. Children need to develop empathy and the ability to read other people's cues accurately. Kindergarteners need to identify their own feelings and understand that others have feelings too. Can other people hold them in their minds? Can other people comfort them? Can I comfort and protect myself and say no? These are the kinds of developmental issues that children should know by kindergarten.

Only about 8 or 9 percent of communication is verbal. Cue reading then becomes essential in social interaction. Cue reading is a sense of mastery, and accurate cue reading can be a sense of survival. Accurate cue reading is also how we make friends and identify enemies.

11. Children entering kindergarten should be able to problem solve. A high self-esteem child will have the ability to see alternatives and continue to build self-worth. Problem solving is being able to

see alternatives and act on them in an appropriate manner. The educational journey is never stalled when one can see alternatives.

12. A child also needs a sense of focus and the ability to pay attention to a goal. As a rule, a child should be able to focus for a minimum of one minute for every year of age. In other words, a five-year-old child should have the ability to focus for a good five minutes on one task and go for the completion of a goal. This requires that the child's brain feels safe and relaxed so that the child has the capacity to think and focus. A child actually has to "feel quiet on the inside" in order to fully pay attention to a goal. Feeling quiet on the inside is equivalent to feeling safe.

13. Kindergarten children should have the capacity to really put their trust in another person. Basic trust is not being afraid, even when vulnerable. It is a belief in others and a sense of hope for the future. Some kindergarteners that I have seen in treatment do not believe that they have a future, a condition resulting from an inability to trust that someone will always be there for them.

14. Children should develop a sense of boundaries. They should have good physical-body boundaries as well as emotional and verbal boundaries. In kindergarten children discover that people cannot be close without good boundaries. In the social interaction life of kindergarten, children will push others away if they do not have good boundaries and constantly touch their stuff. Ultimately, boundaries will be imposed upon children if they do not have their own boundaries. In kindergarten teachers assist children in completing their boundary work by defining space, respecting their names, and confronting trespassing.

15. Kindergarteners should have the ability to differentiate between outside events and inside feelings. I have had kindergarteners say to me, "When people yell at me, I can't think, and my brain shuts off." They go on to tell me that they want to stay by people who do not yell, so that their brains continue to work. These children have understood the concept that inside feelings affect outside events and that outside events affect inside feelings. They also understand that inside feelings determine their ability to think.

16. Children need to have enough confidence to admit mistakes and move on with corrections and then integrate the experience as a valuable learning episode. This requires a positive attitude toward one's self and the ability to correct one's own mistakes.

It is essential for kindergarteners to have mastered a feeling and a belief system based on reparation. What reparation means is that if you break it, you fix it; if you mess it up, you clean it up; if you open it, you close it; if you turn in on, you turn it off; if you don't know how to operate something, you ask for help. If a child can make mistakes and then look for a way to remedy the mistake without feeling devastated, the child will achieve in the educational process.

All sixteen of these essential learning tasks *occur within the context of a meaningful relationship.* None of these competencies develop well or completely outside of good attachments.

Some Basic Assumptions Regarding Education

We cannot educate children to make good attachments or develop good relationships. This is something that has to be caught on an experiential level and cannot be taught in any form of didactic process. Yet education and learning do connect to relating and relationships. Here are seven basic assumptions about those connections.

1. Education can be a change agent but only when it is built upon relationships. For a student it is more important to be known than to know. A child's confidence depends more upon an inner awareness that he or she is known by significant people and much less upon how much the child knows about those people. In a classroom, if I ask each of the children who causes the most trouble, everyone knows the troublemaker's name. However, when I talk to the troublemaking child and ask him or her to name classmates, the child is hard pressed to come up with three of the children's names. The acting out child is often "known" by the rest of the class but does not really belong in a significant emotional manner to anyone. It's not unusual to have an adolescent boy dragged into my office by his parents because of a lack of academic performance in school. Inevitably I discover that the young person, usually about fourteen

years of age, has an IQ in the 140 range but is failing in every subject. The adolescent usually crosses his arms and looks at me defiantly, expressing that he is delighted to see a therapist. I then get his attention by telling him that I can help him get good grades and therefore get his parents off his back if he does exactly what I tell him to do. I tell him that I have no interest in forcing him to do homework or study. Now that his attention is really piqued, I simply say that if he wants good grades within a six-week marking period he has to work diligently to make friends with his teachers.

Some of these adolescents are aghast at the possibility of having to relate to a teacher with whom they have fought over the previous six months. The adolescents who diligently work on my suggestions to form meaningful relationships with their teachers become excellent students out of an internal desire to please someone with whom they have a significant relationship. Getting to know the teacher, caring about the teacher, appreciating what the job entails, respecting the teacher, and picturing the teacher as a caring person go a long way toward academic achievement, regardless of IQ.

2. A second assumption is that no significant learning occurs without a significant relationship. In fact, information that is collected, gathered, and stored within an individual without good relationships ultimately ends up a pile of confusing facts. Brain studies indicate that good cognitive integration requires a low brain arousal level: in other words, a brain that feels safe. Relationships are all about safety and represent contentment and organization in the human life.

When students feel safe, the fund of knowledge and the piles of facts that they learn become organized and integrated within the cognitive process. These children then learn the connection between knowledge, information, wisdom, and knowing what to do with the information.

Significant and sustained relationships teach students to tolerate ambivalence and help them make sense of the world. Children with brilliant minds but no significant attachment figures in their lives often use their brilliance in a disorganized, destructive manner.

3. The third significant basic assumption for learning has to do with external support systems. External support systems such as family,

friends, and mentors correlate directly with success in school. Every student should have someone who touches his or her life.

James Prescott advocates reducing somato-sensory affectional deprivation (SSAD).20 Children who have not had enough good physical touch in their lives often become tactile defensive. When children become tactilely defensive they ward off and push away people and relationships and often do not do well in their school performance. John Steinbeck, the author of the book *East of Eden*, makes a profound statement in his book:

> The greatest terror a child can have is that he is not loved, and rejection is the hell he fears. I think everyone in the world to a large or small extent has felt rejection. And with rejection comes anger, and with anger some kind of crime in revenge for the rejection, and with the crime guilt—and there is the story of mankind.21

Steinbeck held a very negative and certainly hopeless view of humanity; however, I believe he would agree with the statement that an external loving support system is correlated with students doing well in performance areas.

4. It is possible to have a brain and not have a mind. A brain is inherited, but a mind is developed. Reuven Feuerstein, a noted psychologist who studied under Piaget, believes that intelligence is modifiable, not fixed by genetics.22 We know that a brain is a relational organ and develops as it interacts with the environment.

The book *A General Theory of Love* offers "Many subsystems of the mammalian brain do not come preprogrammed" and that "maturing mammals need limbic regulation and limbic resonance to give coherence to neurodevelopment."23 Their theory is that children are born with all of the component parts to a brain, but it has to be assembled and integrated and pieced together by how the environment interacts with that child. Even a conscience is something that is formed as a mental representation of a significant love object.

I believe that John Steinbeck was a great writer but a less great psychologist. He made the statement, "With rejection comes anger, and with anger some kind of crime in revenge for the rejection, and with the crime guilt," but I believe that one can only develop guilt within the context of a relationship; therefore if a child as been rejected and does not have a relationship, very seldom will you see a significant amount of guilt.

5. Actions are more important than words. Haim Ginott stated that the beginning of wisdom is silence, and then comes listening.[24] The brain develops sequentially from the brain stem to the mid-brain and up to the cortex in the first months of life.

In the first nine months of life babies are visually cued with the intent to survive and really do not pay as much attention to words. We learn by our senses: 1 percent by our sense of taste, 1.5 percent by our sense of touch, 3.5 percent by our sense of smell, 11 percent by our sense of hearing, and 83 percent by our sense of sight. If we take this at face value, then actions are much more important than words. And when it comes to obeying rules, requiring structure for the student is an action that conveys love.

6. The opposite of love is not hate. More than anything else, a child is most hurt by being ignored or treated as though he or she does not exist. The opposite of love is "nothing."

The human mind is a representational mind. Humans need some picture in mind of nurturing, loving people in order to feel real, valuable, even identifiable.

An adolescent came into my office and told me that he thought he was a vampire. He stated that he ate like other people, drank like other people, and wore clothes like other people, but when he looked into a mirror he could not see a reflected image. The reason he could not see an image was that he would look into other people's eyes (mirrors) and be unable to see himself. This young man had no significant relationships and very poor nurturing attachment figures. He felt unreal. He was also given to rage reactions and acting out severely against his own body.

Most of the children I see who are unattached would rather be hated if they cannot be loved, because then at least other people would be feeling a feeling toward them. Children have told me that they know what hell is like. Hell is the complete and utter absence of love.

7. The last basic assumption is that education is not the answer for the ills and the problems of the world, because ignorance is not the

problem. Love and a consistent trusting attachment is the answer, because apathy, aloneness, inconsistency, and mistrust are the problems. In a nutshell, "nothingness" is the problem.

The movie *The Never Ending Story* sequences the developmental process of a child who has lost a significant love object, his mother. All through the movie the young boy is being chased by the terrible "nothingness."

Preschoolers must learn to do battle with the terrible nothingness and win, and school-aged children must continue to affirm that the terrible nothingness will not conquer them. Only then do students have free access to the subcortex and neocortex and the complex portion of the brain that develops a thirst for knowledge, impulse control, and healthy personal relationships.

Part 2

The Way It Is

CHAPTER 10

Trauma: Types and Effects with Corrective Measures

Webster's II New College Dictionary defines trauma as "an emotional shock that creates substantial and lasting damage to the psychological development of the individual." My working definition is simpler: trauma is a subjective state of helplessness. The longer this state of helplessness is imposed upon a child or individual, the greater and more severe the trauma is likely to be.

Trauma can occur through personal tragedy or abuse, but it can also be imposed upon the individual by watching someone else be hurt or treated cruelly. Particularly in young children, it seems to make little difference whether the child is the recipient of abuse or if the child witnesses abuse. The net effects of being the recipient or the observer seem to be very similar if not identical in the child experiencing trauma symptoms.

Many parents do not grasp the severity of a child witnessing a traumatic event and do not understand why the child is traumatized if no one has physically hurt the child. Children are traumatized more often than adults think, because children often are in subjective states of helplessness. (The term *subjective* denotes an *internal* perception or feeling, so on a subjective basis I may be traumatized by something that another person views as still within his or her control.)

There are three major factors that impact the child and therefore three types of major traumas: nature, nurture, and fate.

Nature includes what a child is born with, the physical intactness of the child (such as whether the child was premature) and whether or not there are any sensory disorders, such as a hearing or vision problems. If a child is born without any physical anomalies, the child should have a normal stimulus filter. This stimulus filter, also called a stimulus barrier, is a vital part of a child's overall screening and integrating function.

The human child must have the ability to screen out stimuli that may be overwhelming and to allow other stimuli to come through and impact how the child thinks and feels. The human brain then integrates this with the existing fund of knowledge to either feel safe or unsafe. This screening and integrating function seems to process feelings and is primarily a cognitive processing function. It's what helps the baby and the young child feel either safe or unsafe and make a cognitive determination of that status.

The stimulus barrier can best be seen in a very young child, say four months of age. I remember playing with my first grandchild, and while making eye contact with her I could go through all of the antics that grandparents do in a high tone of voice to make the baby smile. The baby would in fact smile, kick her little legs, and play and interact with me. After about three to five minutes of this kind of play she suddenly turned her head to the side and completely shut off the interaction, her attempt to go into a rest cycle after being stimulated.

This stimulus barrier, however, is not completely sufficient for infants, and the nurturant mother also needs to function as an additional stimulus barrier, often up to the age the child is able to walk and sometimes beyond. It is important that the stimulation level be monitored by the nurturant mother in order for the child to develop a sense of safety and protection. These earliest memories are not quickly forgotten.

The second factor that impacts child development is *fate*. Fate includes all of the disasters that children experience and witness, such as a parent's death, a house fire, natural disasters such as floods or tornados, car accidents, violence such as a shooting or a beating, and any other tragic circumstance. These fateful events impact a child's development and cause the child to feel both unsafe and unprotected or to gain a perception of the environment as unsafe or ruthless.

The third factor that impacts child development is *nurture*. This is what a child gets from his or her environment, particularly from the caregivers within that environment. This has to do with whether or not a child has a protective mother or a neglectful or abusive parent. Good nurturing is also impacted by any mental illness in the family and by substance abuse in the family. It is also impacted by the parents' ability or inability to soothe a child.

If there are abandonment or separation issues or dangerous living conditions, this also comes to bear on the nurturant capacity of the caregiver and whether the child feels safe. If the adults in the home have relationship problems and are not able to maintain a constant nurturing environment, this also has an impact on the normal course of development. Donald Winnicott refers to a nurturing environment as a "holding environment"[25] where the mother or father or nurturing love object need to be "good enough," not perfect. Unfortunately, the nurturance that many young children get actually predisposes them for a real sense of trauma.

Correlating roughly to these three factors that impact child development are three major types of trauma in a child's life. Correlating with nature is *genetic trauma*, when children are born with neurological problems, brain chemical imbalances, or severe allergies or pollutant reactions. Genetic trauma would also include children who are severely dyslexic and have real learning disabilities, mentally impairments, fetal alcohol syndrome, prenatal cocaine exposure, or genetic mutations. Sometimes genetically traumatized children will have physical handicaps such as vision problems, hearing loss, loss of a limb, or severe muscle coordination difficulties such as found with cerebral palsy. They could also have severe sensory integration problems and be unable to interpret the environment's cues. Any child born with a mental or physical difficulty could be said to have genetic trauma.

When a child is born genetically traumatized, the energy investments that should drive a normal stimulus barrier to keep the child calm are shifted to a compensatory ability that the child can do as compensation for the anomaly. Children who are genetically traumatized seem to be less able to screen out noisy environments, integrate former knowledge and experience with current experiences, and generally make sense of the world around them. They are less able to compartmentalize and hold historical information for future reference.

These children have to stay on hyper-alert more often to compensate for the physical difficulties. These also seem to be the children who are more susceptible to what a teacher called "spazzing out."

Correlating with the impact of fate on child development is what I would call *acute trauma*. Acute trauma generally is sudden and of short duration, such as a tornado, a flood, a fire, an accident, a drowning, or any kind of natural disaster. It could also be called shock trauma. Acute trauma could also be caused by witnessing tragic events such as abuse or murder or even a parent being hauled off in handcuffs to jail. Physical, sexual, or verbal abuse could also qualify as a fateful event and an acute trauma.

This brings us to the impact of nurture on child development. The trauma that correlates with nurture is called *cumulative trauma*. Masud Khan coined the term in an exquisite article found in the journal *The Psychoanalytic Study of the Child*.[26] In that article Khan talks about all of the seemly small and insignificant events that children go through that actually are quite traumatizing but go unnoticed, except by the child. These could be situations of not being supervised, a child getting lost in a store, a baby rolling off a changing table, constant job losses within the family, or constant and multiple moves. It would also include things like a primary caregiver constantly switching live-in boyfriends, adults giving the child sharp criticism daily, or adults handling the child roughly. Constant parental temper tantrums, constant tension with the household, and verbal threats given to the child also qualify for these small accumulations of trauma.

In 1978, when I was working at the Grand Rapids Child Guidance Clinic in Grand Rapids, Michigan, we came across an inordinate number of children who our child psychiatrist would diagnose as post-traumatic stress disorder children. When we looked at these children's social and developmental histories, we could not find any genetic trauma issues such as a physical or mental anomaly; nor could we find any acute trauma such as accidents or natural disasters. What we did find were children who were being cumulatively traumatized by a daily diet of parental temper tantrums and a combination of all of the things previously mentioned. We even found that certain childrearing patterns could be classified as cumulatively traumatizing.

A childrearing pattern of teaching a child to handle trauma by giving them trauma is actually traumatizing. We came across parents who would want their children to learn how to handle life circumstances and so they would purposely set the children in harm's way. These parents wanted to teach their children to swim by pushing them off a dock or to teach their children not to be afraid of the dark by making them walk home in the dark or to teach their children not to play with fire by allowing the children to be burned. Parents might also smash toys if they weren't picked up or hang out wet bedsheets in the front lawn to embarrass children whenever they wet the bed. One parent wanted to teach his child to tie his shoelaces. (The child knew how but thought it was "cool" to leave his shoelaces dangling.) The parent snuck up behind the child and stepped on the shoelaces, tripping the child so the child fell flat on his face. This was explained by the parent as a way to teach the child a lesson. However, the parent was teaching the child trauma!

Maybe the myth that parents can teach their children to handle trauma by giving them trauma comes from the medical model of vaccinating children against a disease by giving them a small dose of the disease so that the body builds up immunity. Psychological and emotional trauma do not fit into the medical model, and this kind of "nurturing" often leads to a trauma type of bonding with the parent as a result of chronic victimization where the child has little or no power. Over a number of years, children subjected to these cumulative trauma events will look like they are traumatized and could actually exhibit post-traumatic stress disorder symptoms, not the least of which would be hyper vigilance, which could then garner the child an attention deficit disorder diagnosis. Cumulative trauma will teach the child that the world is not safe, parents cannot or will not protect them, and they live in a hostile environment where they must be hypervigilant, stay on the move, be ready to fight or throw a temper tantrum, act tough, don't trust, be suspicious, and at all cost be in control.

A child will have either the power of love in a soothing relationship or the love of power. Pity the child who is born genetically traumatized, then raised in an environment that cumulatively traumatizes him or her, and then encounters acute trauma in a severe life circumstance. It is amazing to see the resiliency of children who have in fact endured all three types of trauma.

CHAPTER 11

The Psychological Effects of Trauma

Trauma does damage or severely effect children's perception and behavior. However, there seems to be a direct correlation between the amount of damage done psychologically and at least six influencing factors. The more of these factors a child has, the more the child will be damaged and the longer the recovery, with more corrective work needed in order to help the child regain an emotional equilibrium.

The first factor that will affect the emotional or psychological damage is the intensity of the violence or the trauma. It will make a difference if trauma is continuous or if it is intermittent with rest periods in between traumas where the child is able to feel safe. If children have continuous trauma they tend to maintain a high brain arousal level and constantly stay hypervigilant, making rest impossible.

The second factor is the type of trauma. A sexual assault, because it is so personal, would tend to cause more damage than a non-sexual physical assault. In cases of neglect, parents who don't care about the child and refuse to nurture do more damage than passive neglect, where the parents seem absentminded. Generally speaking, personal types of trauma produce more damage than general types of trauma, such as being involved in a car accident.

Another factor that influences the amount of damage psychologically to the child is the duration of the trauma. When a subjective state of helplessness continues over a long period of time, children seem to suffer more emotional damage. Their basic sense of control and safety in the world is severely impaired when the state of helplessness goes on and on.

A fourth factor correlating with emotional damage is the relationship of the traumatizer. If a child is traumatized by a parent, the emotional psychological damage done seems to be greater than if the child is hurt by a friend or acquaintance. This has to do with the trust factor and children's belief that their parents should be their protective agents rather than agents of harm. Trust is severely damaged when someone who is supposed to love and protect you turns on you and hurts you. The more intimate the relationship between the two parties, the more damage is done.

A fifth factor has to do with the age of the child at the onset of the traumatization. The older the child at the point of onset, the better off the child is, because of the capacity to think through, process, and rationalize the root cause of the traumatization. Children who are very young (0–5) have a difficult time figuring out and rationalizing the abstract thought process that needs to go into why a trauma happened and why certain adults did not or could not protect them.

The last factor that correlates with the amount of damage done within a child has to do with whether or not physical threats were used. A ten-year-old boy reported to me that when his father got drunk he would haul out his 44-magnum handgun and put one bullet in the chamber. He would then spin the cylinder, cock the gun, put it to the child's head, and ask the child if he "felt lucky." This type of physical threat of great bodily harm evokes in the child the fear of death and certainly impacts the amount of damage that's done to the child because of the extreme sense of utter helplessness.

Trauma produces psychological effects. Listed here are fourteen of those effects, as well as the signs of these effects of trauma and potential corrective measures.

1. Blurred Boundaries

Trauma often smashes any sense of separation between the traumatized person and other people. It is absolutely essential to have good boundaries, and when a child is traumatized these boundaries are compromised, making the child feel much more vulnerable.

These could be body boundaries, emotional boundaries, and mental boundaries as well as spiritual and moral boundaries. Trauma smashes boundaries and creates in the child the expectation that everyone will now be a "smasher" of boundaries.

The observable signs of poor or blurred boundaries are that the child will tend to take things, no matter who they belong to. These children tend to touch everything. They have no respect for privacy, and they expect no protection of their own bodies or their own belongings, so they quickly cry foul when their boundaries are violated. These children are very egocentric—the world revolves around them—and after a severe traumatization seem truly surprised when told about protecting other people's boundaries as well as their own. In an extremely genetically traumatized child, such as a child who is born autistic, there are virtually no body boundaries evident.

I once saw a little boy about the age of seven who was severely autistic. When I went to the waiting room to bring him to my office, he asked if he could hold my hand. I offered him my hand, which he quickly grabbed onto, and then he asked, "Am I a part of you now?" He believed that because he was touching me he was melded to my body and had become an extension of me. Children who have had their boundaries smashed by things like physical or sexual abuse live in constant fear, because when there are no boundaries, one never knows who will violate your space or your body.

Corrective Measures

Defining space can help the child who is cumulatively or acutely traumatized. Define what is your body and what is his or her body. Define what are your objects and what belongs to him or her. Continuously recognize and protect physical belongings and validate the concept of ownership. There is a real paradox here when it comes to ownership and sharing. If you really want a child to share, stress the fact that the child owns something and in fact does not have to share it. Along with validating ownership, one should also confront any trespassing. Ask the child if the objects they are touching or taking belong to them, and require that the child ask permission.

Another corrective measure for blurred boundaries is to reassure children that they have a "place." Reassure the child that he or she will get a turn speaking or a turn playing. For severely traumatized children I have gone so far as to write a quick note to the child that says I am guaranteeing that he or she will get a turn. That way these boundaryless children are reassured that I will hold the boundaries, and they actually have something to hold in the form of a piece of paper that guarantees that they will have a turn or a place.

Another corrective measure with blurred boundary children is to respect their bodies. If a child has been traumatized, respect for body boundaries is absolutely essential. Always ask these children if you may touch them or hold their hands or shake their hands or sit by them. Showing that kind of respect for boundaries is a powerful modeling example.

A few years back I inadvertently traumatized some of my co-workers by making an office change without their permission. I was a program director of a large agency that laid off many of the personnel during the summer months and then reemployed them in the fall. One summer I decided to move some offices to different locations, but, rather than contacting these people and asking permission, I went ahead and had their desks and personal effects moved. When they came back in the fall, everything was already done. The trauma that this caused was unbelievable. (And yes, I should have known better.) Boundaries are an important aspect of people's identity and sense of value as well as their sense of security.

Having boundaries also means respecting the child's name. It is pretty standard for me to say to a child, "I know your name is Andrew, but what may I call you when we are talking?" That child will often say, "Call me Andy." On occasion I get a smart-aleck youngster who tells me to call him "Pipsqueak" or some other goofy name, at which point I simply state that I want to respect his boundaries, and part of respect is calling him by a name that is socially acceptable and not derogatory.

After a traumatization it is not unusual for the traumatized person to start over, building up boundaries. Any support and help that can be given to a child who is working on boundaries will profit not only the emotional development of that child but also the people who come in contact with that person.

2. Faulty Reality Testing

The second psychological effect of trauma is "faulty reality testing." There is an old acrostic that says that F-E-A-R is False Evidence Appearing Real. Traumatized children often have a difficult time testing out what is real and what is fantasy, what is truthful and what is false. A severely traumatized child often starts to doubt reality and often then falls prey to additional trauma because of the impaired ability to test out reality.

The observable signs of faulty reality testing include things like time distortions and not knowing which events happened in what sequence, or not knowing what happened yesterday or what could happen tomorrow. Traumatized children often find it difficult reading cues from other people and ask questions such as, "Are you mad at me?" or "Do those kids like me?" They have a difficult time knowing whether children are laughing at them or at something else. They will ask if something they did hurt someone or did not hurt someone, because of their lack of reality testing.

These traumatized children believe in a "law of repetition": if something happened once, it can and will happen again. Once the child is traumatized, the child tends to believe in personification much more and starts attributing danger to inanimate objects. These children also tend to become overly superstitious and connect events to things that they were doing.

I met with a child who had been playing video games when his father beat up his mother. The child never played another video game, and when I asked him about it, he sheepishly admitted that he didn't want anyone else to be hurt. His assumption was that if he started playing video games, this might cause someone to get beat up. The more a person is traumatized, the more likely he or she will regress to early childhood thinking and start using preschool thought processes.

Corrective Measures

It is important to be patient and to encourage the child's questions. Spell out expectations as specifically and concretely as possible, and always talk in concrete language, never using slang abstract language or euphemisms. Children who have been extremely traumatized do not abstract well and therefore fail to interpret euphemisms or slang language and will go back to a regressed, almost preschool kind of thought process.

Additional corrective measures for faulty reality testing include defining what hurts people and what is normal, validating feelings and validating sensations. It is extremely important to validate a child's feelings, because it helps the child develop a natural protective system. A child who has had his feelings validated will know that if he is approached by a pedophile and told that sexual play is not bad, he must run for help. A child who has rarely had his feelings validated, however, is always questioning what is real and what is not real and is much more at the mercy of people who do not have the child's welfare at heart.

Another way to help children with faulty reality testing is to be willing to entertain their superstitions but to cast doubt on them. Take time to explain why superstition may not be valid and also cast doubt on the feeling that once something happened it's repeatedly going to happen. We should always thank these children for asking questions and checking out their reality even though it may seem self-evident to us.

3. Loss of Basic Trust

The third psychological effect of trauma is a rupture of basic trust. The observable signs of this effect include an exaggerated startle response and a general restlessness in the child. Often they are gaze aversive and can even become tactile defensive in spite of often being "touch hungry." After the trauma, however, they want to be able to control all stimulation, including touch, and so they find new ways to gain touch. I have seen children gently back into people and allow themselves to rub up against a safe significant love object. However, when this person would inquire if the child would like hug, the child would quickly take off. They may also gain touch by jumping on other children, not so much as a malicious act but in an attempt to make contact.

After the trust has been ruptured with other human beings, children often go into parallel play rather than cooperative play, and poor socialization results. These children often go into what I term a "paranoid stance" which looks like a young person walking around emotionally constricted. Their muscles are tense; they seem to be holding back; they're wide-eyed and scanning the room for danger. The child is in a state of physical and emotional discomfort.

Another observable sign is the need to be in absolute control. There is only one letter difference between the words *attach* and *attack*. If children do not have the ability to attach, which requires trust, they will become attacking and demand absolute control. Often these children only want to play with younger children because they perceive them as safe. Change and transition are often difficult for children lacking trust, and they are quick to fight and quick to take offense.

Non-trusting children will also hoard objects or food, almost as if they cannot trust others to provide the basic needs that they require. These children also need proof of everything and often demand, "Show me!" A child who has lost trust in people expects to be tricked and self-soothes by sitting by the door or going to school early to maintain a position of perceived control.

Corrective Measures

A corrective measure for a non-trusting child is consistency. The rules and expectations stay the same, and as much as possible the responses stay the same. It is often helpful for these children to be matched up with one special person to build trust rather than to expect a non-trusting child to develop relationships with a number of people. When the routine has to be changed, it is important to inform the child of changes as much in advance as possible to help the child predict and thereby feel safe within the environment.

Personal integrity is also important as a corrective measure. In other words, adult body language needs to match verbal language, because children who had their trust smashed quickly perceive when adults say one thing and actually end up doing another. The survival brain of the human is visually oriented, and therefore children visually pick up cues as to the actual intent of the upcoming action.

With children who are extremely non-trusting it is important to describe virtually every move. Let the child know you are approaching and what you are going to do next, such as reach for a pencil on his desk. Children who have had their trust destroyed need to start at a primitive level of being able to read body cues and predict everything that is going on.

Another way to establish or reestablish trust is to set up rendezvous situations. The non-trusting child might take a risk and ask the adult if the adult will read him or her a story. To set up a rendezvous, the adult would say, "I would love to read you a story; meet over at the beanbag in five minutes when the big hand is on the twelve." Once the rendezvous has been set, the adult needs to be sure he or she is at the rendezvous point. Numerous rendezvous throughout the course of the day help non-trusting children to experience promises kept.

It is important to the child to have a name and for the adult to use it. It is also important for the non-trusting child to learn the names of others, because it is virtually impossible to trust someone who does not have a name. It can also be helpful to assign the traumatized child as a helper to a younger or more vulnerable child. That way the child who lacks trust is vicariously treating himself or herself by helping a more vulnerable person to gain trust.

In a school setting there should be no field trips for the first six weeks of school so that the child can acclimate to the classroom and develop a feeling of security. Any major change throughout the school year with a child should be met with an anticipatory guidance program (AGP).

4. Disruption of Regulation of Self-Esteem

A fourth psychological effect of trauma is the disruption of the regulation of self-esteem and self-empathy. Self-empathy is the ability to proactively soothe oneself; after a traumatization the child tends to feel helpless in the ability to feel calm.

One observable sign of a disrupted regulation of self-esteem is the child who only sees one solution to a problem and cannot seem to be able to grasp alternatives. Such a child could go to a computer class and see that all of the computers are being utilized. The child cries, "All the computers are being used; I don't know what to do," at which point the child sits down and is unable to move.

A child with high self-esteem will instead start to look at options and alternatives.

Children who have been traumatized often call themselves "stupid" and rip up their own papers whenever they produce something that may be of high quality. These children do not expect comfort or help and certainly do not know how to self-soothe. They also tend to mock others who are in pain or who get hurt within the classroom, and they themselves often have a high pain threshold.

The one soothing mechanism these children seem to have is the use of rage. Children who have had their self-esteem disrupted use rage as a soothing mechanism because it represents self-empathy and a relief from the tension. It also represents a sense of control based on their perceived inability to control the inside of themselves and their feelings.

Corrective Measures

It is important to validate any feeling the child has. This does not mean that children should be allowed to act on every feeling. It is also important to try to hold eye contact. Low self-esteem children tend to shy away from eye contact, although some cultural characteristics call for a child not to make eye contact with an adult. It is important to be the "perfect mirror" when the child accomplishes something important. The teacher or the adult might clap or stand in awe of the child and let the child know the work is appreciated. Dr. Heinz Kohut said, "You are not real until you see yourself as real in the eyes of another person."[27]

The environmental attitude is also extremely important for these children. When the environment affirms that mistakes are for correcting, the child becomes less afraid to make a misstep.

Another corrective measure for low self-esteem is to be empathetic with the child. This translates into paying attention to every hurt that the child demonstrates. Elementary school teachers should start the year with no less than a thousand Band-Aids available in their class cupboards. If teachers attend to every hurt, the children will actually become hurt less and be able to help themselves, soothe themselves, and help others. Empathy is a contagious factor.

It is important to thank children whenever they do something appropriate. In his wonderful book *Teacher and Child*,[28] Dr. Haim Ginott talks about appreciative praise, which is basically thanking a child rather than evaluating the child and saying that the child is "good." It is important for children to label themselves on the inside as "good" people rather than for adults to label them on the outside as good or bad. This can happen if we praise the child appreciatively by saying thank you rather than saying, "That was a good job."

Additional corrective measures include getting to know the child's strengths, fears, and favorite things and becoming attached to the child as much as the child can tolerate. Attachment has a curative effect on any child and requires that one know the child.

5. Identity Struggles

Self-concept or identity is a fragile and somewhat tentative thing for many children. Younger children have not learned to give self-reinforcement or to classify as unimportant those areas in which they cannot perform. They rely on others to form their sense of identity. If others are untrustworthy to do this job, it makes it that much more difficult for the child.

As children grope around for a sense of who they are, traumatized children often find security in a negative or a bad image. At least if they have a bad image they are able to define who they are. This explains why children go to great lengths to reinforce a negative self-identity. As much as they try to reinforce that sense of self, it behooves the caring adult to, by repetition, convince children that identity is not linked to something "bad."

A child struggling with identity is often surprised at his or her own feelings. These children have a difficult time making decisions because they don't know what they want and often are caught in role-diffusion: not knowing if they are the kid or the adult. Children who have gone through the trauma of sexual abuse often have sexual identity issues, wanting to switch genders and imagining that if they had been the opposite sex people would not have hurt them.

Another observable sign of identity struggle are children who dislike their anatomy, for example, boys who refuse to stand up while urinating or who want to take off their body parts and exchange them for someone else's. Particularly in this area, the traumatized child is different from the grief-stricken child. Trauma distorts identity, whereas grief rarely distorts identity.

Corrective Measures

It is important to set the roles straight and define the child's role as a child, or as a student, or as a son or daughter. Tell the child that someday he or she will get to be the teacher or the parent. Encourage same-sex mentors for elementary-aged children as a way for them to accept their sexual identity.

It is important that no teasing take place about any part of the child's body. The adult involved with the child should develop a mental picture of who this child is and who this child could become in the future. Then if the adult acts as if it were already true, the child seems to unconsciously pick up the positive picture and strives to conform to the mental representation that is in the adult's mind.

It is important to attempt to make each child, particularly children struggling with identity, a "special person." "Special person of the week" is good within schools, but I also encourage teachers to get permission from the child and the parents to carry around the child's individual picture. At any given time during the day the child can ask the adult if the adult has the child's picture, and the adult can produce it. This metaphorical sense of holding the child seems to enhance a sense of positive value and sense of identity.

6. Obsessive Thought Process

After a traumatization children often worry about minutia: safety things like whether the smoke alarm works, if the windows have locks, if the teacher knows the police department's phone number, and where all the fire exits are. Often there is a need for perfection, as if something bad would happen if the child weren't perfect. Superstitions are common, and children often panic if a specific routine is not followed.

Traumatized children will actually talk audibly to themselves at the expense of conversation with others. Compulsions such as having to hang their coat on the same hook are not unusual, nor are expressions of fear of death.

Children who have been traumatized often feel guilty, which is another attempt to be in charge rather than to feel impotent and a victim of destiny. These children often ruminate over small things like whether their hat looks okay, their pants are too short, or their hair is combed in the right direction. These all seem to be themes of acceptance.

Corrective Measures

The corrective measures for the child with these obsessive kinds of thought processes include orienting the child as much as possible throughout the day. Orient the child in terms of place, time, and person. Ask a child where he or she is at any given moment in order for the child to click back into reality orientation.

Constant reassurance that the child will be safe is always good, as is a focus on the real present rather than what the child is trying to do, which is to control the future. Always address the fears that a child has as a theme rather than try to deal with each individual fear separately. Remind the child that he or she is safe. It is difficult for these children to play spontaneously and actually have fun, because this represents letting go of control. It may be important to play with the child and facilitate the play in order for the child to tolerate a sense of internal risk.

It is important to address magical thinking. Children might hold the magical thought that if they somehow had been better, the trauma would not have taken place. Tell these children that people do hurtful things because *they* have problems, not the child. Encourage children to take small risks like playing and interacting with others, but appreciate the anxiety that this evokes within the child who worries about being safe and therefore in control.

I like to tell children struggling with these obsessive thoughts a metaphorical story and will ask the child to help me with the story. I might say, "Once upon a time there was a boy who needed to use the very same coat hook at school every single day. Why do you think that boy needed to do that?"

The child may produce an answer such as "So he could feel safe."

I would then continue the story by saying "When the boy was in school the teacher kept him very safe, but the boy still wanted the same hook. Why do you think that was?"

The boy might respond, "Just in case." I then talk to the child about wanting the future to be safe and say that we control the environment as much as possible so that in fact the future will be safe. However, I impress upon the child that to have fun, to play, and to live is to take some risks.

I finish the story with the boy starting to take small risks and finding out that he can be really happy.

7. Intolerance of Ambivalence

Children who have had good attachment and good bonding with significant love objects have the capacity to tolerate ambivalence and should have this capacity in the preschool era. When a child, no matter what age, is traumatized, the capacity to tolerate two different feelings is lost. Especially if it is a personal traumatization such as physical or sexual abuse, the child seems unable to hold opposing feelings about one person. Traumatized children have had their trust smashed and their object constancy severely damaged and must start over to rebuild the capacity to tolerate two different feelings toward one person at the same time.

Children unable to tolerate ambivalence often see people as either all bad or all good, depending on the actions of that person. They quickly idealize someone but at the first misstep quickly turn and see that person as all bad. They go from friend to friend and playmate to playmate, unable to hold a consistent relationship because they cannot tolerate opposing feelings.

They often develop fantasies of being able to "erase" people. One little girl said to me, "I disappear you" when I had made her unhappy. The inability to hold two different feelings also affects relationships with inanimate objects. If they make a mistake on a paper, it is not sufficient to erase the mistake; the child will rip the paper up and get a new one. Everything in life becomes either all good or all bad.

The inability to hold friends because of an intolerance of ambivalence leads to the trauma friendship cycle (see figure 3). In the trauma friendship cycle the traumatized child is constantly searching in hypervigilant mode to find a friend. Traumatized children are not good socializers, so they pick somebody to test whether they will give acceptance. When these children find someone who will tolerate them, this newfound friend immediately becomes their "best friend." They will over-idealize this person and become very possessive of this person's time.

They constantly worry over loss, and, because of their possessiveness, the "ideal friend" starts to look elsewhere. The traumatized child starts to panic over the potential loss, becomes aggressive, and decides to become the rejector before becoming the rejectee. When the friend finally dumps the traumatized child, the traumatized child may become hyperactive and aggressively controlling to overcome feelings of helplessness. The traumatized child then temporarily isolates himself or herself in order to soothe into equilibrium and then starts looking for a new friend by picking, prodding, and poking others. Because these children cannot accept that their friends could like them and also like someone else, they cannot tolerate a constant relationship.

Figure 3 (see next page)

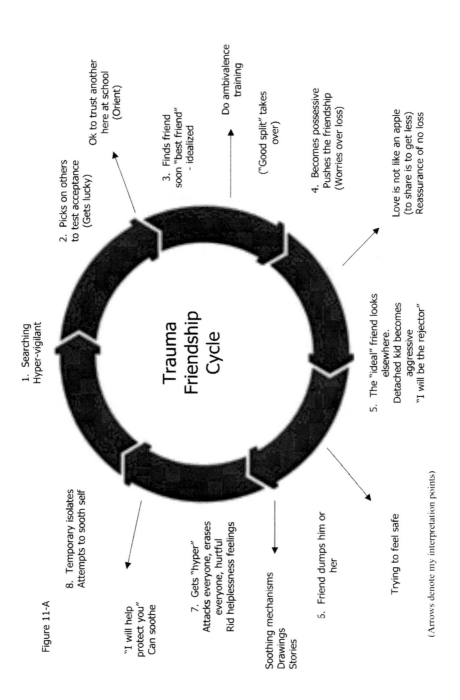

Figure 11-A

Trauma Friendship Cycle

1. Searching
Hyper-vigilant

2. Picks on others
to test acceptance
(Gets lucky)

Ok to trust another
here at school
(Orient)

3. Finds friend
soon "best friend"
- idealized

Do ambivalence
training

("Good split" takes
over)

4. Becomes possessive
Pushes the friendship
(Worries over loss)

Love is not like an apple
(to share is to get less)
Reassurance of no loss

5. The "ideal" friend looks
elsewhere.
Detached kid becomes
aggressive
"I will be the rejector"

Trying to feel safe

5. Friend dumps him or
her

Soothing mechanisms
Drawings
Stories

7. Gets "hyper"
Attacks everyone, erases
everyone, hurtful
Rid helplessness feelings

"I will help
protect you"
Can soothe

8. Temporary isolates
Attempts to sooth self

(Arrows denote my interpretation points)

145

Corrective Measures

To help the child become tolerant of contrasting feelings, point out to the child at every opportunity that sometimes good feelings are evoked and sometimes bad feelings are evoked toward the same person. When children become angry with me I point out that an hour ago or yesterday they thought I was the most wonderful person on earth. I then ask them if they are really angry with me. When they say they are, I ask them if I am the same person as I was yesterday. This often baffles these children, and occasionally one will say, "No, you're a different person." I say that I am the same person but they have different feelings toward me. Often children need time to simply think about that and process it.

I also sometimes use a cutout doll when I talk with a very young child. I draw a picture of a doll on a piece of paper and name that doll the name of the friend (let's call him Jimmy) with whom the traumatized child is having difficulty. I ask the child to tell me five things he or she "used to like about" Jimmy and five things he or she now hates about Jimmy. I write these attributes on the paper doll, and when we're done I cut the doll in ten pieces, with each piece having an attribute. I then mix up the pieces as if it were a puzzle and pull out the bad attributes, leaving only the good attributes on the table for the child. I then ask the child to put Jimmy back together. The child will tell me that Jimmy can't be put back together because some of the pieces are missing. I tell the child, "You are exactly right. In order for a person to be a whole person, you have to have all of the pieces. Sometime pieces of people are bad, and sometimes pieces are good, but it's all one whole person. This is a helpful exercise in bringing the splitting together. On occasion this may make the child anxious, however he or she will then just block it out.

Other corrective measures include being constant with the child, having a regular framework of rules, and offering yourself as a protective shield when others pick on the child. Suggest to the child that the goal of being angry is to really solve the problem of how to be close. Talk about remembering people as whole objects with both good and bad characteristics. It may help to show them the trauma friendship cycle and actually plug in names. The capacity to tolerate ambivalence is one of the most important ego functions that a child can develop.

8. Reduced Problem Solving

When a child is traumatized, the emotional energy that the child could use for cognitive processing in abstract thinking seems to be taken up by keeping the brain in a high state of arousal and alert. This tends to reduce the ability to solve problems, process and integrate, and make sense of what is going on around them. The observable signs of this effect are that the child is easily confused and does not want to make decisions. Decisions, in fact, are quite panic provoking, and children often become scared when asked to make them.

These children also look for quick fixes; a number of children ask me for medication because their "brain doesn't work well." Older elementary kids often strike out aggressively, and it is not unusual for them to run away from home, at least for short periods of time.

Children who have been severely traumatized forget things and have short-term memory problems. Things don't seem to register with them, and they have a difficult time figuring out what is meant and picking up cues accurately. Traumatized children have difficulty remembering and solving problems and are often mistakenly diagnosed as ADD when in fact a diagnosis of posttraumatic stress disorder would be closer to the truth.

Corrective Measures

The adult should keep the choices limited to a maximum of two alternatives and continue to remind the kids of their successes. Teachers can keep positive experience (PE) books. Every time a child has a success, write it down in a notebook. Do not give the books to children, because kids inevitably lose these books and therefore seem to "lose their successes." The adult should maintain the role as "bank vault" of the child's successes, making entries into the PE book and allowing the child to look at it and read it at any time.

Adults should always appreciate the fear that children have of *being* wrong, not just *doing* wrong. If children have been severely traumatized recently, it is not unusual for the adult to have to function in the role of "alter ego," choosing alternatives for them and functioning as a model during a crisis period. Once the child stabilizes, the child can start making decisions from two choices; however, during the intensity of a trauma it is perfectly fine for the adult to function as the alter ego.

9. Increased Fears

Traumatized children express increased fears, including fears of loss, rejection, or intimacy. They are also literally afraid to feel!

The observable signs of increased fears include what I would call "jealous lover syndrome." These kids need to know where the adult is at every second, and once the adult is out of view they start to panic.

They also regress in their capacity to form memory. There seem to be three levels of memory in a child: recognition memory, when the infant needs to see the actual object in order to recognize it; evocative memory, which requires an association in order to evoke a picture of the love object or the person that's known; and volitional memory, when a child can call up the picture of a soothing, safe loved person by just thinking about that person. When a child is traumatized, the increased fears push the memory ability to the lowest level, and the child needs the object within sight to feel safe. These memory stages can be rebuilt within the child, but the child has to have a consistent safe love object who is willing to form a significant attachment in order to do so.

Other observable signs include resisting closeness for fear of losing someone, and denying all feelings. In order to develop the capacity to be alone, it is necessary to be alone in the presence of a significantly loved person. Because of the fear factor, traumatized children need to learn how to be alone all over again, and they do that by attaching themselves even physically to the significant adult. Once they again feel safe that this loving figure is going to protect them and stick by them, they are willing to venture out and incorporate the significant love object's mental picture in their head, which they can carry with them everywhere. Carrying a picture in your mind of a safe person is the ultimate soothing mechanism.

I warn adults about the actual emotional pace that they use to help a child become less fearful. Many well-meaning adults smother the child with affection, only to find the child vehemently rejecting them. When I talk to these parents I use the metaphor of a child who has been starving. It is not possible to feed this child large amounts of food, because the stomach has shrunk to such a small size that the child will throw the food back up. In the same way, children who are starving for safety and love should not get massive doses right off the bat, because they will have to push it away out of their own fear that this is too much too soon. Once the child has learned that the significant love object is going to be constant and can "feed" the child in small doses, the child will take larger and larger amounts of love and nurturing until satisfied.

Corrective Measures

Accept the child's pace of getting close, and reassure the child of a consistent presence even when unseen. A transitional object can be helpful for children who are really fearful, even something as simple as a business card.

Children of a fairly young age should be able to listen and integrate some interpretation of their fears. It is not unusual for me to say to a child, "You seem really nervous about something, and I want you to know that it's okay to talk with me." Adults should liberally make interpretations with children, even if they are wrong, because children love to set adults straight, and the child is often willing to correct the interpretation.

Other corrective measures include encouraging children to be artistic in their expression with things like drawing, writing poetry, and the use of clay. Stop night terrors in children by having children draw as much as they can remember on paper and suggest that now the images and the thoughts are on paper, outside of their heads, where they can be contained. Writing brief notes and writing in a journal are also wonderful ways to combat fears by bringing them outside of the head and into the front of the child's vision, where the child can feel a sense of mastery.

10. Introjected Voices

The psychoanalytic literature calls voices that are heard on the inside "introjects." Children who have been traumatized, particularly by a significant person within their environment, often hear these introjected voices.

The observable signs of bad or faulty verbal introjects will be noticed when children start to repeat on the outside some of these voices that they hear. These voices can say things like "You're stupid; people don't like you" or simply "You can't." These children are unwilling to exhibit any of their performance abilities, and showing off for others, even in a good way, is out of the question. These children certainly would not stand up in public and perform.

Traumatization seems to surface all of the bad and faulty voices on the inside of children. When I hear children say, "I can't," I ask them to add at least one word to that phrase—the word *yet*. It is imperative to implant a sense of hope in children.

To correct faulty verbal introjects, make an intense deal out of the child's achievements. Write them down in a PE book, and applaud the child loudly when he or she has done something well.

Use a little neuro-linguistic programming with the children to teach them to "change their state" to interrupt the voices on the inside. When a child hears a negative "I can't" voice on the inside, ask the child to change his or her physical state: if sitting, stand up; if walking, run, etc. Movement has the capacity to change chemical responses in the brain, and when children change their physical state, they can interrupt a negative voice on the inside, at least temporarily.

Ask the children to talk over a negative voice that they hear. If they're hearing and feeling that they cannot do something on the inside, ask them to say out loud on the outside that they can do it. Often a combination of music and walking around helps the child to, at least temporarily, erase negative verbal voices on the inside.

In a classroom it is also helpful to build a community where all the children support each other, and when one child says that he or she can't, other children can chime in and tell this child that he or she can do it and that they are willing to help.

11. Scary Mental Representations

Mental representations are basically pictures on the inside that we can see in our mind's eye. When a child has been traumatized, the good pictures on the inside are preempted by scary pictures. The observable signs are that children report seeing and feeling scary things in their heads (called flashbacks) and generally are unable to hold the good, safe pictures on the inside for any amount of time.

These children are visually hypervigilant, their eyes darting from one end of the room to the other. They alternate between being clingy and avoidant, and if they are at all artistic they draw war scenes and fights and use up the red color to draw blood and body parts. These children never seem to feel safe, always expect the worst, and can exhibit real depression.

It is extremely important for children to have soothing, solid, safe pictures of people who love them on the inside. Children can never relax and never feel safe when they do not carry around with them a soothing picture of loving human beings.

Corrective Measures

It is essential to promote mental pictures of safe people. Ask the child to make an actual photo library of safe, loving people, such as grandparents, coaches, good friends, or loving teachers. These children should draw pictures of safe people from memory to practice holding pictures on the inside of their heads. It may also be good for children to carry around transitional objects from safe people, such as a key ring from Grandpa or one of Mom's gloves.

To put safe pictures on the inside of children's heads, try to get them to associate the loving and safe people with odors. Using all of the senses to promote safe pictures helps to establish that association and links the safe past with the current struggles. If there is no "safe past," find current safe people to hold mentally.

In her book *Too Scared to Cry,* Lenore Terr talks about recapitulation and revision.[29] Recapitulation is when a child has in mind a very scary picture of what happened during a trauma and reworks the pictures in order to master it, hence using revision to feel in control. A seven-year-old girl once told me that she saw her mother hitting her four-year-old brother with a belt. Her brother was screaming, and she told me she grabbed the belt from her mother's hand and hit her mother with it. After a few more sessions, the story changed to the girl hiding in her room and covering her ears.

It is therapeutically important for helping adults to accept the child's version and then help the child feel safe until, with enough distance from the actual trauma, the child starts to voluntarily tell the helper the truth. This "recapitulation and revision" process is a way to cope with the intense fear and the awful mental pictures that get planted in children's heads during an episode such as this. It is perfectly okay to ask children what they can picture inside of their heads and then to change those pictures to pictures that are soothing and protective.

12. Regression in Defense Mechanisms and Coping Skills

Traumatized children tend to regress in their usage of appropriate defense mechanisms. At young ages children exhibit defense mechanisms of clinging, avoidance, splitting things into all good or all bad, acting out, denial, and projecting what they do or did onto other people. These are all legitimate defense mechanisms, but they are not the most effective in resolving any kind of trauma situation.

As children get older they learn to wait, anticipate, and channel their aggressive energies into things like sports or displace their anger onto beanbags or soccer balls. They also use their own intellectual abilities to rationalize and make sense of why things happen, and they also have a better ability to repress bad situations. After traumatization children will lose their ability to use these higher levels of defense mechanisms and go back to the primitive clinging and avoidance and denial type of protective devices.

Going back to the use of these primitive defenses is an attempt to manage the untrustworthy, inconsistent internal and external love objects, mainly the adults. Children seem to fantasize that if they go back to the primitive defense mechanisms they will have and maintain ultimate control. Unfortunately, primitive defense mechanisms tend to stay with the child the more the child uses them.

Corrective Measures

Adults need to encourage children to identify their ability to cope and defend against anxiety. Additional corrective measures would include being honest and trustworthy with the child and sharing with the child how the adult handles things like anger, frustration, fear, and embarrassment

Teaching the child how to breathe is also essential. Children who are fairly primitive in their range of defense mechanisms tend to be shallow breathers. The shallow breathing seems to help a child stay at a hyper-alert level; however, it also tends to hype the child up to the point of not being able to identify with a stronger adult who knows how to handle anxiety.

Another good corrective is to role-play with the child what to do in certain situations. The capable adult can take the role of the child and demonstrate both verbally and physically how the adult would walk through an anxious and scary situation by using higher levels of coping skills, such as rationalizing the problem or displacing it physically into an activity.

13. Desire for Absolute Control

When children are traumatized, everything becomes scary. They want control over their environment, over people, and over their emotions in an attempt to keep away bad feelings and scary thoughts. These children tend to be bossy and demanding, and they quickly perceive that people are rebelling against their wishes. They can easily escalate into aggression when they don't get exactly what they want. Interestingly enough they tend to avoid groups, because it is very difficult, if not impossible, to control the whole group.

These children hate transitions and change, because they have to reestablish a sense of inner balance and control as well as external feeling of control. They often present a stoic countenance, smiling and laughing very little. These kids often sit by the door, which is a place of power, because they can escape easily if they want to, and they usually get to school before anyone else does, in order to feel safe.

A first grader told me that if he gets to school before anyone else, in his own mind he claims the classroom as his own domain. He then watches the children come into the classroom and slowly integrates them into *his* space. He thus maintains control, at least in his fantasy, over the entire situation. If he should happen to come to school late, it's too scary, because he has to walk into a room that he does not "own," and twenty-five pairs of eyes are looking at him.

Corrective Measures

Children who need this kind of absolute control can be given options within a consistent acceptable perimeter. It is perfectly okay to partner with the child to find ways to feel in control and safe in an appropriate manner. It is important that the child know that feeling safe is okay; it's a matter of how one goes about it.

The child may benefit from a "ready room" or a "ready area" when coming into school so as to feel safe and comfortable before integrating into the group. Children who need tremendous control with their peers need to hear that absolute control with their friends actually hurts them in establishing good friendships. These children tend to have a very poor ability to monitor how their actions turn people off and away from them. It is essential for adults to walk through these situations and verbally explain what happens along the way to the child and how excessive control actually contributes to a sense of isolation and a lack of peer relationships.

Children who exhibit a tremendous need to be in control are not exhibiting this behavior because they think it is fun. This kind of controlling behavior is usually born out of a deep and terrifying fear. These children often feel that unless they are in control, something awful will happen, first of all to them, and also to anyone they love.

14. Isolation of Affect

Affect means feeling. Children who have been traumatized often take their feelings and completely bury them in order to feel as if they can survive. The observable signs are denying pain, denying caring about anything or anyone, and having a blunted range of feeling. The intensity of feelings seems to be on a continuum; if a child consciously or unconsciously shuts off all feeling of sadness or pain, the child also unwittingly shuts off the capacity to feel joy and pleasure. This produces a child with a very limited range of feelings and hence a stoic child who doesn't have much of an expression. Anther observable sign is a child who has a difficult time feeling happy.

I had one brilliant twelve-year-old tell me that he had "feeling leprosy." When I asked him to explain, he said that leprosy is a central nervous system disease that shuts off feelings in various body parts; therefore when the person gets a scratch or injury it goes unattended because it's not felt. The scratch or injury gets infected with bacteria, and the bacteria spreads, and eventually paralysis and wasting away of muscle occur, causing grotesque deformities. The boy admitted to shutting off feelings but also knew the consequence would be that he would not attend to himself and that ultimately he would become paralyzed and deformed. This young man realized that shutting off his feelings was a protective device but involved a cost to his whole body and to his interactions with others. The cost was in fact so heavy, he regarded it as an emotional deformity.

Corrective Measures

To bring out and make safe the feelings of children who are isolating, adults should notice small feelings that the children have. Point out that it is risky to feel, but if they start out small, maybe they can allow themselves to feel greater and more intense feelings. Be ready to help the child compartmentalize (i.e., box up) the feelings if they become too intense.

In her book *Handbook for Treatment of Attachment-Trauma Problems in Children,* Beverly James offers the child a "feeling bag" to put the feelings in, including screams, if the child would like to.[30] It is also therapeutic to separate feelings from actions, something that younger children find difficult to do. By separating feelings from actions, children are less afraid to act out their feelings because then feeling them is not same as acting on them.

It is essential to reassure children that if they feel they will not die or go crazy. Children as young as four and five years of age believe that if they relate verbally the intense feelings that they have on the inside, they will go crazy or even drop over dead.

Read emotional stories to these children, because they can start to feel outside of themselves and vicariously through these story figures. They may need to start to feel in the third person first. Sometimes I encourage skits and plays that have to do with feelings and human interactions as a way of introducing and keeping feelings safe.

Once children have experienced fears in the third person, suggest that it is okay to feel some of these feelings in small ways in their daily lives and interactions. This again is a process of introducing feelings by degree. Patience is a virtue when it comes to helping children feel their feelings for real and giving them an impression that they will live through the process and come out a whole and intact human.

CHAPTER 12

Soothing Mechanisms

Children can be traumatized quickly, but they can also adapt quickly and learn to soothe themselves. Dr. Bruce Perry has a wonderful Web site for Child Trauma Academy (www.childtrauma.org) where he talks about a hyper-arousal continuum, which is a continuum of adaptive responses that the child makes to threats. Dr. Perry lists five mental states of increasing intensity when a child is faced with a threat: the calm state, a state of arousal, the alarm state, fear, and finally terror. Dr. Perry associates each one of those states with different cognitive functions and different uses of the brain and talks about the adaptive response children make to the environment. He also explains the different relational responses to people that children have at different levels of feeling states or mental states.

In the state of calm there is a good reciprocal interaction between the child and the adult. All body states—vision, hearing, smell, and tactile functions—are operating at an optimal level during a calm state. There is also good sensory integration with these functions, and the emotional and physical relationship between the child and another person can be warm, affectionate, and safe feeling. Children may say, "I feel like people are real, and I can trust what they say."

In Perry's next state of arousal the child starts to become hypervigilant and scans both the room and people for potential threats. The senses become heightened, and in this state children may become light sensitive and slightly tactile sensitive. Children start relating to others in a more instrumental manner.

Allow me to give you a silly but perhaps helpful example. If you were with a group of peers discussing any given topic, and there was a good interchange and a good relational communication going on, one would see others as whole objects and real people and enjoy the reciprocal give-and-take reactions. If, however, a wild (foaming at the mouth) wolf appeared, looking extremely hungry, your relationship with others in the room would change drastically. The friends you were previously chatting with and relating to as valuable human beings would suddenly become potential steaks that you could throw to the wolf to save yourself. Your peers would no longer function as valuable relational objects but would become instruments of survival. It is not unusual for a child in trauma to switch rapidly from functioning in a reciprocal interactive way with children to start using the other children as instruments to get what he or she wants.

In Dr. Perry's third mental state, that of alarm, children become even more sensitized to interaction, to the point of their skin seemingly becoming sensitive to touch. It is unwise for a teacher to grab a child in this state because of the hyper-alert level that the child is in; the grab would be perceived as a vicious attack by the adult. The attachment level and the attachment wish to other children as well as to adults are reduced in this alarm state, and the child is hyper-vigilant and hyper-reactive. Children may develop selective hearing in this state because they are tuning out all non-critical information and listening for any potential threat, such as the shuffle of feet or a threatening tone.

In Dr. Perry's next mental state of threat, fear, children attempt to soothe themselves by defiance and acting tough. Muscles are usually constricted to ward people off. I've seen children use the defensive structure of identification with perceived aggressors to feel safe. This function is the child deciding to be the aggressor before anyone else has the opportunity to become a danger to the child.

In the final state of terror the brain functions are pretty much on automatic and the cognitive functioning is pretty much reflexive. In terms of relationships, children tend to be in primitive survival mode, which basically is no relationship at all to others but simply an attempt to save themselves. Children in terror mode might huddle underneath a teacher's desk and scream, hiss, or snap at people who attempt to pull them from beneath the desk.

When these children calm down, they are able to verbalize that in terror mode they do not take in their whole environment but simply see what their brain classifies as dangerous parts: huge hands coming in to try to get them or feet trying to kick and stomp them. It is rare that the child would see the whole person.

Talking to a child in this state is not necessarily going to be soothing. In the terror state a child's cognitive functioning is not able to process, abstract, or integrate what is going on. Allowing the child a brief quiet time before talking helps the child to self-soothe and reconnect to the thinking process.

All people have their own unique soothing mechanisms. I personally enjoy chewing on plastic straws that I collect throughout the week when I buy coffee. I find the oral gratification quite soothing, and it keeps me from eating or smoking.

Many traumatized children lack soothing mechanisms, and these children can be helped by adults who assist them in finding soothing and coping mechanisms that suit their personality and their environment so the children can learn to function as their own soothing agents when a soothing adult is not available.

Soothing mechanisms are extremely important to children who have what Dr. Perry calls sensitized brains. Dr. Perry talks about "neuro-response sensitization," which is an actual brain change as a result of a sustained threat and trauma. Dr. Perry states that the brain is "use dependent." If a threat happens repeatedly over time, the brain reorganizes itself by increasing receptor sites for the alertness chemicals to handle the specific trauma. If this continues over a number of months, the neuro-responses become sensitized, and the pattern is ingrained into the brain. Once sensitized, the child can react with a full-blown act of aggression even when triggered by a small external stimuli.

On occasion a child will tell me that his or her teacher yells and screams at him. The teacher will deny yelling, although the teacher may admit to raising his or her voice to a student, especially about a disciplinary action. This is what Dr. Perry calls brain sensitization or neuro-response.

Let's say eight-year-old Jimmy is shaken awake by his mother, who starts screaming at him to get out of bed, find his clothes, find his homework, and get his breakfast. She is still screaming at him when she pushes him off to the bus for school. This happens every morning for a number of months, and then one day Jimmy walks into the classroom and carelessly throws this coat behind his desk. The teacher observes that and slightly raises her voice, saying, "Excuse me, Jimmy. You need to pick up your coat." The ever-so-slightly raised voice triggers all of the neuro-responses in the brain, because Jimmy has a brain sensitized to the sound of screaming. Jimmy's response is to scream at the teacher, "Why are you yelling at me?" Dr. Perry's sensitization patterning indicates that a small raised voice can trigger all of the alertness chemicals within the sensitized brain so that Jimmy, in his head, hears screaming from his teacher when in fact there was no screaming.

Figure 4 contains a list of thirty-four soothing mechanisms. Some are self-explanatory, and others require a bit of explanation.

Figure 4

Soothing Mechanisms List for the Classroom Child
(Adapted for potential use with ADHD child)

1. A consistent framework.
2. Transitional objects.
3. Encourage recognition of "signal anxiety."
4. Anticipatory guidance programs (AGPs).
5. Keep record of successes (PE book).
6. Emphasize boundaries and ownership.
7. Juice box.
8. Assume "they would if they could" instead of "they can but they won't."
9. Teach "what should I do now" rather than "why did I do that."
10. Use simple, sequential, concrete language.
11. Say "thank you" a lot.
12. Practice breathing (cup hands over nose and mouth).
13. Competing soothing stimuli (rocking/music, hum to self or quietly talk).
14. Surgical brush.
15. Soothing smell.

16. State changes.
17. Clay play.
18. Drawing.
19. Tight coat.
20. "Smoothie."
21. Thumb wrestle.
22. Reparation (relieves guilt).
23. Rub under collar bone.
24. Picture cards of emotions.
25. "Fidget" toys.
26. Tug-of-war.
27. Carry small bottles.
28. Safe voice on tape.
29. Hold what's next.
30. Increase air circulation.
31. Reassurance photos.
32. Orient child.
33. "Unfold ears."
34. Sorting objects.

1. A consistent framework: A consistent framework includes rules, consequences, and routines: using the same entrances and exit doors as well as having the same bus driver, teacher, aide, and lunchroom attendant. I once was consulted by a school district that rotated bus drivers because it was cost effective for each driver to know every other driver's route. Because the children would get a new driver every month, no relationship was formed with drivers, and aggressive bus behavior was reaching dangerous levels. I suggested that the district assign the bus drivers the same routes for the rest of the year. It took only twelve weeks to see a significant drop in bad bus behavior. No other variable was changed.

2. Transitional objects: This includes objects from home—a toy, a key ring, or other small articles that remind the child of a consistent, loving, safe person. Transitional objects can also be objects that can be used within the school setting when moving from one activity to another.

Number 27 on the list, "carry small bottles," is a soothing mechanism that I learned from a preschool teacher who was having a difficulty with children moving from their classroom to the gym play area. The anxious and traumatized children would find the move extremely upsetting and would inevitably pick fights or go running down the hall with the teacher in pursuit. The teacher noticed, however, that when children had to carry weight to the gym area they seemed much more calm and soothed. She filled plastic detergent bottles with water and asked the children who had a difficult time making a transition from the classroom to the gym area to carry a bottle in each hand to the gym area. This worked marvelously.

Another transitional object is number 31 on the list, "hold what's next." Sometimes children become very anxious anticipating a transition such as a bus ride home. One teacher found that if she handed the child a small toy bus five minutes before the child was to board, the child seemed more calm, almost as if the bus in his hand gave him an illusion of having control over the bus transition.

3. Encourage recognition of "signal anxiety": The term *signal anxiety*, coined by Anna Freud, refers to behavior signifying anxiety, such as darting eyes back and forth, fidgetiness, taking rapidly, bouncing the knee, or other movement or twitches. Everyone experiences signal anxiety. It is helpful to teach even young children to observe their own body movements, their own actions, and their own feelings. If a six- or seven-year-old child can notice leg bouncing, pencil tapping, or some other behavior as anxiety triggers or signals, the child can move to a calming posture or move into a soothing type of behavior.

Children need to recognize when they start to develop signal anxiety so that self-care can be administered before the breakdown of their cognitive processing and before they get aggressive because of the anxiety. When a child is able to recognize anxiety, raise his or her hand, and ask permission to go out into the hallway get a drink of water, this becomes an effective mechanism to guide children in impulse control and to feel safe in their own actions. Often children have no clue that they emit signal anxiety and therefore need to be taught what their body is telling them. Children can become amazingly aware of their developing anxiety and can find ways (with adult help) to quickly route the action appropriately.

4. Anticipatory guidance programs (AGPs): AGPs are visualization processes that can be helpful and soothing for students. The exquisite soothing human brain is the only brain that can actually plant a memory of success *prior* to the actual event.

I was called by a second grade teacher to help her because she dreaded taking a field trip to the planetarium. She had in her class three or four traumatized children who were anxious, leading to aggression whenever there were major changes in the classroom. I suggested that she do an AGP with the class the day prior to the actual field trip. The teacher set up the chairs to look like bus rows, and the children were guided in mental imagery all the way from the bus ride to the planetarium, through the big doors of the building into the projection room. The teacher described in detail what they would see and what they would experience. She talked about the room being dark and looking up at the ceiling and seeing the stars and constellations. She went into quite a bit of detail, asking the children to close their eyes and imagine that they were actually there. After doing that they again in visualization got back on the bus and imagined themselves riding back to school, walking up the sidewalk, and coming back to class. The teacher stated that everyone was safe and then held a discussion on how they liked the planetarium. The anxious students were able to talk about what they had "seen," and everyone on the class thought it was "cool."

The actual trip went well the next day, even for the anxious students. AGPs are absolutely essential for traumatized children, who need to be able predict, control, and feel safe no matter what goes on in their environment or who changes it.

5. Keep record of successes (PE book): These allow adults to be a "bank vault" of good memories for the child. The parent or teachers always keep possession of the PE book while allowing the child unfettered access to his or her book. Even at the end of the year when the child is moving on to the next grade, the teacher should retain the book. It is not unusual for a child to go back to "visit" the previous year's teacher, and if the teacher is able to haul out the PE book and show the child the successes from the previous year, it is very encouraging to the student.

7. Juice box: A juice box can be an emergency tool when children become anxious, aggressive, and out of control. Sitting in the corner, sucking a juice box and indulging in that kind of oral stimulation, is actually quite soothing for the child. After the child has finished drinking the juice box, when the child is calm, it will be possible to have a discussion with the child.

8. Assume "they would if they could" instead of "they can but they won't." This is self-explanatory and simply represents a positive attitude towards children who do not perform prescribed tasks.

9. Teach "what should I do now" rather than "why did I do that": Trauma negates cognitive processing. When traumatized children say that they can't produce something, they are telling the truth. At that point children need more hands-on help to feel safe and to allow their cognitive processing to reach its full potential. It is essential that the relationship between the teacher and the child include two mental images of the child: who the child is now, which includes the belief that the child is working as hard as he or she can, and who this child can become.

It is also important for the environment to be one in which mistakes are accepted as a normal process of life. Problem solving is the important issue, not whether something is right or wrong. This includes mistakes in behavior as well as academic mistakes.

Within a classroom situation, to create a sense of belonging, put children's names and pictures on the wall, both their present reality as well as pictures of who they are going to become in the future. A sense of belonging includes the rituals of saying hello and good-bye on a consistent basis throughout the school year. Something as simple as saying hello and getting that greeting recognition and saying good-bye and planting the picture of the person in their heads is extremely soothing and contributes to a sense of belonging and of security and safety that is essential to many of our children if they are to succeed.

10. Use simple, sequential, concrete language.

11. Say "thank you" a lot: Soothing mechanisms include using language that is concrete and understandable to the child and also appreciative rather than labeling. As Dr. Haim Ginott said in his book *Teacher and Child,* labeling a child "good" actually increases the child's dependency on another person to continue to uphold the label. The difference between saying "thank you" to a group of children or calling that group a bunch of angels is the difference between working hard and developing internal motivation or having the children become anxious and break out in fighting to prove that they do not deserve the label of "angel."

12. Practice breathing (cup hands over nose and mouth): Traumatized children tend to be shallow breathers. Sometimes it is soothing for children to cup their hands over their mouths and noses and breathe deeply as if breathing in a paper bag. The rebreathing of a child's own carbon dioxide offers the child some brief respite, possibly enough for the impulse control system to regain a sense of security. (This is very similar to number 30. Providing children more air can feel soothing.)

14. Surgical brush: Brushing himself or herself on the arms and exposed skin with soft surgical brushes can help the child to self-soothe.

15. Soothing smell: For some children the classroom is their safest environment. Each classroom should have a distinct smell, such lavender, rose, jasmine, or even baby powder. These tend to be calming smells, as opposed to lemon, cinnamon, or mint. If the teacher has a bit of potpourri in the corner of the classroom, the child quickly orients to the room through the olfactory sense and often calms down quicker. It may help to use the same calming smell on the bus so that once the child is picked up from home the bus triggers a sense of security and safety.

16. State changes: Ask students, "Where are you right now?" in order to orient them into the environment that is safe and nurturant. This is particularly helpful for traumatized children who live in chaotic households or households that have screaming adults and constant bickering and badgering happening on a daily basis. Orient the child to the classroom verbally.

I suggest that the children in their home environments oftentimes have to put on a survival suit. In order to survive in a "lion's den" one has to become a lion. They therefore have a lion suit on and will snarl and snap with the best of them. When they come to school, however, the teacher metaphorically asks the student to take the lion suit off because this is a different environment. Do that by asking the child, "Where are you now?" The child orients to the school's "safe" environment, and one can almost see the child remove the "lion suit."

Five or ten minutes before the students are ready to be dismissed, teachers should tell the students that there is ten minutes before school will end. This may cause the child to start to put the lion suit back on, and the child's behavior for the last ten minutes often is aggressive and inappropriate in anticipation of returning to a difficult home environment.

19. Tight coat: When some young people get out of control and feel anxious, they need to physically feel contained. I recommended that the teacher have a "security coat" in the classroom. It generally is a coat that has a zipper and is either a full size or a half size smaller than the size of the most anxious child in the classroom. When the child becomes anxious and starts to spiral out of control, it may be helpful to tell the child to put on the security coat. When the child zips the coat it hugs the child when human hands are too anxiety provoking. The child can wear the coat for a while and then has the option to put it away when self-control and security are restored.

20. "Smoothie": At the point that a child starts to spiral out of control, the teacher tells the child to go get a smoothie. The children should have all been instructed that a smoothie comes from a pump-top hand cream bottle; they are to pump out enough hand cream to lather all over their hands and to begin rubbing it on any exposed body parts, such as hands, face, and neck. The physiological component of ringing their hands while spreading the hand cream releases the body's natural dopamine, one of the most soothing chemicals that the body generates.

21. Thumb wrestle: When a child is feeling aggressive, this is a safe outlet; plus it allows a safe way to hold the child's hand.

22. Reparation: This may not sound like a soothing mechanism; however, when we require children to make reparation for something that they have done wrong, particularly a behavior that was hurtful, it soothes the child's guilt and actually enhances future positive behavior.

In a first grade classroom I observed a boy smack a girl on the arm rather viciously. The little girl cried out in pain. I told the young man that it was not appropriate to hit; however, now that he had done it, he needed to fix it. He rather perfunctorily turned to the girl and said, "I'm sorry." I told the young man that "I'm sorry" did not cut it and that he needed to fix what he had done. He informed me that he could not take the hit back, so I suggested to him that there might be other things he could do to relieve the pain.

After a few seconds of uneasy quietness the little boy decided he could get a paper towel, soak it in cold water, and hold it on the girl's bruised arm, which he did, holding it on the girl's arm in a most loving manner in total silence for about two minutes. I asked the little girl how her arm was feeling, and she acknowledged that it was better and that the cool water from the paper towel seemed to take away the sting. I told the young man that he had fixed what he had injured but would still have to take the consequence of playing in a different area for that play period.

I am a big believer in helping children feel some healthy guilt and also learn that the best way to relieve guilt is to make reparation or, in kid language, "fix it." A little guilt goes a long way, so be careful not to pour guilt on a child, but heaven help our society if children stop feeling the guilt of hurting someone or letting a loved person down.

33. "Unfold ears": Instruct children to take their own ears in their hands and see if they can smooth out and unfold the natural folds in the ear. Obviously they can't, but in the process they are rubbing their ears, which is a soothing mechanism for many children.

Children have a myriad of soothing mechanisms naturally. I strongly suggest that every adult carefully observe children and respect the soothing mechanisms that they have unless they are obviously harmful. Sometimes it is helpful simply to legitimize the child's existing soothing mechanisms!

CHAPTER 13

The Etiology of Rage

Rage is very different from anger. Rage is more violent, more instinctually survival-oriented, and has a furious intensity. Next to rage, anger looks controlled.

The etiology, or root cause, of rage begins in infancy. Infants and children quickly feel unsafe. Masud Kahn, in his article "The Concept of Cumulative Trauma,"[31] talks about the development of rage, and this will be the basis of my formulation on the etiology of rage. Kahn states that it takes approximately ten days after an infant is born for that infant to figure out whether or not he or she is safe based on the predictability of the environment, touch, response time, whether cues are picked up, verbal stimulation, and the reciprocal interaction between the caregiver and the baby.

Many babies become over-stimulated during this first month of life by fighting parents, loud environments, being hauled to multiple caregivers in the course of a week, and being treated like a commodity rather than a viable, extremely perceptive human infant. If, in this first month, the child starts to feel alone and unprotected, the baby can start to formulate a picture of the environment as uncaring and unnurturing.

If the unnurturing and unprotective environment continues into the second month, the child builds up what Kahn calls a "need tension." The baby does a lot of scanning, looking for help, looking for soothing, and exhibits distress through sleeplessness, having gas pains or colic, rigid muscles and hyper-alertness, an exaggerated startle response, hiccups and gagging responses, and being a fussy eater.

Our English word *neglect* comes from a French and ultimately a Latin word *negligere*. Literally translated, *negligere* means "not to touch"; when we neglect a child it is usually because we do not touch the child in a warm and nurturant manner.

If the neglect continues into the third or fourth month, the child starts to develop a perception that he or she is a separate human being. Kahn calls this "premature separateness." In the normal developmental sequence, children are not supposed to feel completely separate until about the eighteenth month of life! Margaret Mahler states that it takes approximately eighteen months for the child to feel connected and well attached, which is the child's primary task in those eighteen months.[32]

The next eighteen months, until the age of thirty-six months, the child works on being separate and independent. The child who starts to feel separate at four months truly is way ahead of the developmental sequence and will pay for this premature separateness.

These prematurely separated infants show lots of signs of beginning rage and fear of hurt or deprivation. They are visually directed, reaching out randomly, and often self-stimulating. They have jerky motor movements and disorganization in their overall activity. They often put up verbal protest to any kind of new image or odor or temperature changes. These little babies look like they are frantically trying to adapt to the environment around them.

If this kind of neglect continues through the fifth and sixth months of life, the child begins to feel even more separateness. The child also starts to develop rage and starts to express it through screaming, kicking, and other raging reactions.

By the time the child hits seven to eight months of age we do not see specific stranger anxiety in these children. (One only sees stranger anxiety with a well-attached child, because to be afraid of strangers means that you have a good relationship with a specific love object.) These eight-month-old babies begin to show signs of depression, with very little range of affect and poor sleeping patterns. Lack of sleep creates sunken dark circles around their eyes. These babies start to believe that what and when they get fed is much more important than who feeds them. (A well-attached baby would rather not eat if there is no relationship with the person feeding him or her.)

At ten months the child will start to project rage onto other caregivers rather than neutralize it. Rage is neutralized in a relationship and in a close attachment. In a closely attached child, the child may get angry, but the caregiver soothes the child, which neutralizes the anger so that it doesn't progress into rage. In a non-nurtured unattached child, the caregiver starts to become the "enemy." The baby begins to become even fussier and more demanding. If the caregiver responds back in a rageful manner, this only confirms to the child that the environment is unsafe, uncaring, dangerous, and undependable.

If anywhere along this continuum a significant love object such as a nurturing adult comes alongside of this baby and starts to nurture and attach to the baby, this progression toward rage can be neutralized, and the baby can be saved from a life of feeling abandoned and enraged. A nurturing reciprocal interaction within a relationship neutralizes rage and helps the child to recognize other people as humans, just like the child is. The longer this progression of a non-nurturing, non-soothing environment continues, the more difficult it is to convince the child that rage is not necessary to survive.

The development of rage has nothing to do with culture or social-economic class. Income makes no difference. The very wealthy family can neglect a child; an impoverished family can nurture a child. The key factor is not income level, social-economic class, culture, or religious orientation. The key factor is attachment and a caring, reciprocal interaction.

By eighteen months, if the child continues to be unnurtured and unprotected, the child will actively start to live independently. This includes the use of rage when needed. The lack of trust is easily exhibited in his or her tenuous relationships with other people.

These children have a very poor memory of any kind of soothing objects, and when they develop language it is used primarily as a weapon to get their needs met and not to control their impulses. These children lack the internal conscience to help modify impulses.

At twenty-six months of age, a child raised in a non-nurturing, non-safe environment is now walking and talking and seen as aggressive, non-trusting, and hurtful, with a lack of empathy.

The child's view of the world is "I am the center of the universe, and I have to get my needs met, so get out of my way." Other people are either all good (if they provide them with what they want) or all bad (if they don't).

At about twenty-six months the normally developing well-attached child often has temper tantrums: the "terrible twos." Well-attached children have tantrums out of indignation over the adults no longer bowing to them and giving them exactly what they want. When an adult is consistent with rules and discipline, children recognize that they have to share the world with other human beings and will continue to form other attachments.

The unattached, over- or under-stimulated child who is not nurtured does not have normal temper tantrums. They have *rage reactions*. If others do not help them get what they want, they will perceive it as a threat to survival, because they are already separate human beings and see themselves as having to take care of themselves. Their reaction then is one of rage, which often is expressed in what I call "murderous rage," wanting to exterminate the person who is blocking their path to get what they want.

Kahn calls these violent, rageful children "emotional preemies" because they have had to prematurely separate and be unprotected by the adults in their environment. Rather than being nurtured through development, these children are frightened through development and do not know the security of protective and well-attached adults.

At the age of thirty-six months, these children often displace their rage at their unprotective parents and lay it on other people, acting out against peers or other adults. The raging child recognizes the need for the primary caregiver, at least for food, and therefore the rage gets projected away from the original non-protectors onto child caregivers, preschool teachers, and others.

If these children do not get nurturing, attaching, soothing adults interacting with them, rage continues and intensifies as they get older. Fast forward to kindergarten and to first grade, and one can see which children have the need to protect themselves by their own rage. It becomes a situation where a child will either "attach" or "attack."

At a workshop for a group of teachers and parents a number of years ago, a young woman gave me this poem, entitled *Rage*, that she wrote while listening to me.

In this world we become, looking around my life's undone.
No one to care, no one to see
I'm crying out loud, help me please.
I fend for myself, you are not my friend,
You give me what I want and that rule may bend.
I hate you; I love you, why are you here?
I've never had any one to hold me dear.
You try to stop me, this is a mistake,
I'm on my own; you give I take.
I may act younger or too old for my age,
From five days old I have begun this rage.
You think you can control me or tell me what to do,
Ha that's funny, I will get rid of you.
I continue to look for a hug or a kiss,
I could ask for some love or I could make a list.
If you are wise, you can change my ways,
You could nurture and love me for the rest of my days.
If you continue to leave me and to let me go,
Where my rage will take me nobody knows!

People often ask me, "What's the big deal about attachment, anyway?" The big deal can be summarized in seven points:

1. It neutralizes aggression.
2. It develops impulse control and a conscience.
3. It develops empathy and the capacity for empathy.
4. It promotes basic trust.
5. It promotes brain dendrite and neuron development.
6. It establishes identity.
7. It allows for exploration of this world without excessive fear, because there is someone safe on the inside.

Is attachment a big deal? Yes, it is a big deal!

CHAPTER 14

Cathexis Versus Decathexis

As one works in the field of therapy one integrates and compiles many thoughts and theories from the books and articles that are read. The concept of cathexis and decathexis as well as the idea to formulate a cathexis scale all came from a 1984 journal article entitled "Intermittent Decathexis—A Type of Parental Dysfunction," written by Robert A. Furman and Erna Furman.[33] It is a timeless article and very relevant to our current crisis of children not being well attached.

In this chapter I am going to use the word *cathexis* interchangeably with the word *attachment,* and *decathexis* interchangeably with the term *detachment.* I actually prefer the word *cathexis* because, as the Furmans describe it, it is a constant energy investment in a human object, and it is an investment of psychic energy in a mental representation. The word *cathexis* therefore stands for a solid attachment and investment in not only another real person but also that picture of the real person inside of one's head.

This is an intense investment in a whole object, meaning the good points and bad points of another person. It includes an emotional electrical charge of energy excitement in the presence of such a loved person. Teachers who have "eyes in the back of their head" have cathected their students enough that they can anticipate and predict the students' movements. Cathexis in another person is a good thing!

Paul Minear, in an article entitled "Eyes of Faith," said, "For a child it is more important to be known than to know. The ground of his confidence depends less upon how much he knows about his family than upon the inner awareness that he is known by his family."[34] The word *cathexis* denotes such an investment. As the Furmans stated, "We invest in others as we invest in ourselves, and we invest in ourselves as our original caretakers (parents) initially invested in us." The investment process or the cathexis process is very much a learned process and is not a biological given.

The prefix *de-* means the opposite of, or the removal of, something. *Decathexis* means removing the energy and the investment in a person. When a friend or a teacher or a parent decathects a child, often that person is avoiding a competition between his or her wishes and the needs of the child. Often parents have a difficult time avoiding the displeasure of the delay in their own gratification of their wishes, and the parents feel they must pursue their own interests, which often means the child is going to be treated as if he or she does not exist.

Even the best of parents at times decathect their children. A mother receives a phone call from her best girlfriend and starts to cathect in her mind to this friend, formulating a picture in her mind of this friend and discussing topics they enjoy. All the while the two-year-old is watching Mom and feeing energy being taken from the child and invested in the caller on the phone. The two-year-old then goes to the kitchen and pulls open a cupboard, removes a bag of flour, and starts to dump it all over the floor. When Mom sees the child making a huge mess, she quickly tells her friend that she has to go and hangs the phone up to deal with the child. The child now feels the mother is back to paying her the attention and is satisfied that the spreading of the flour has done the trick. It's almost as if the child in her own mind says, "I'm being decathected right now with Mom's friend on the phone and that makes me feel terrible. I'm going to get my mommy back and have her recathect and invest in me by doing something that I know will make her hang up the phone."

Fathers do this too when they come home and read the paper. The wife or the children often perceive the lack of investment as abandonment. Short decathected periods are at times needed by parents or teachers to replenish their own energy and needs; however, when dealing with children who worry about losses, particularly a loss of investment, it behooves the adult to either busy the child with a satisfying or pleasurable activity or find a surrogate substitute to stand in while the adult takes a break.

Decathexis can be very functional. Decathexis is adaptive in the mourning process when someone dies. At the death of a loved person we are forced to withdraw the physical investment in that person because the physical being is no longer with us on this earth. That investment, however, is put into a mental representation with all of the memories we have of that loved person. We therefore decathect the body of a loved person and recathect to that person on the inside of our head with memories and mental pictures. It is possible therefore to let go and to say good-bye to a loved person, especially if that person is significantly cathected, because the energy investment simply transforms a body attachment to a mental attachment.

If, however, the loved person is not significantly cathected, the mourning process can take longer and is made up of a cathecting process. This is one reason why mothers with stillborn babies need to touch and hold the baby for a short period of time to make that child real. Once the mother makes the child "real" through a cathexis process, that mother can say good-bye and still retain the "internal baby."

The process of decathexis is also developmentally important in what might be termed as "object removal." This is particularly true of little boys who must developmentally decathect from Mommy and identify with an adult male. The young boy can only do that if he cathects to an adult man, and once that cathexis and identification have taken place, the child is then free to cathect to Mommy in a new way and subsequently later on in life to fall in love with a female. Decathexis is therefore functional in the developmental process.

Decathexis is used defensively when children do not have consistently cathected love objects. Sometimes parents establish what Furman calls "intermittent decathexis," which means to invest in the child for short periods of time and then withdraw that investment when they get busy with other activities. This would be the "football dad" who is greatly invested in his son on the football field but the rest of the week is so busy that he treats the child as if he does not exist. The excruciating pain of intermittent decathexis is too much for many children to handle; therefore they tend to completely withdraw and even express hate and violence to the significant love object. Decathexis therefore is used as a defense for the off-on again pain of inconsistency.

I have often seen young children attempt to protect themselves or regain a significant love object's attention by threatening decathexis. Four-year-olds will say to their parents, "You better be careful; you almost lost me" when they are in a busy mall. The child sometimes threatens, "I'm going to run away," which is really a threat that the child is going to decathect the parent. The child's own greatest fear is what is used to threaten others.

I have also seen children try to protect themselves from decathexis by a parent who doesn't know how to attach to a child. While I was interviewing a seven-year-old girl, it became obvious that this little girl was extremely precocious and in fact had reversed roles with the mother. This girl was mothering her mother and doing so in order to be taken care of. When I wanted to set up another appointment, it was the girl who took the Franklin planner out of her knapsack and was ready to write down the date and time of the next appointment. This girl was protecting herself from being decathected by her own parent by actually parenting the mother, who was then more able to accept this little girl having value. This little girl was soothing herself by being the mommy but also and more importantly pleasing the mommy and keeping some of mommy's cathexis or investment by providing her own nurturance. Consistent decathexis often leads to abuse and neglect.

The Furman article on intermittent decathexis, the writings of Ainsworth on attachment theory, and Donald Winnicott's good enough mothering theory contributed to the formation of my working parental cathexis scale (figure 5). Each end of the continuum is an extreme, and the optimal place to be is in the middle. That middle zone Ainsworth would call "secure attachment"[35] and Winnicott would call "good enough mothering."

The top of the cathexis scale describes parents, and the underside of the continuum describes how children respond to the corresponding behaviors of the parents. At one end of the continuum is severe decathexis, while the other end of the continuum is what I term "hyper-cathexis." Complete decathexis or detachment in one's child is as destructive as hyper-cathexis. In hyper-cathexis, the parent breathes the child's air before giving it to child, and because this constitutes a denial of a separate identity, it is as destructive as total decathexis, which is also a denial of a separate identity and value and individual worth.

Figure 5 (see next page)

Cathexis Scale

Formulated by Phillip D. Hamberg
© 2000

Parental Cathexis

3rd degree Decathexis	2nd degree Decathexis	1st degree Decathexis	"Good enough" cathexis	1st degree Hyper-cathexis	2nd degree Hyper-cathexis	3rd
Severe	Intermittent	Casual	Held in "mind"	Doing with	Doing for	Anxious
Deprivation	Decathexis	Forgetting	Good object constancy	Very controlling	Cuts off mastery	Preoccupation
Not real	Narcissistic	Overcommitted	Boundaries empathic	Sees child not separate	Psychosomatic	"Other me"
No memory	Extension	Traumatized	Volitional	Be my fantasy	Anxiety/hostility	Obsessive
	Recognition	Evocative			Not sensitive to cues/signals	

Child Responses to Parental Cathexis

No conscience	Aroused state	Apathy	Makes friends	Apprehensive	Attention getting	Self absorbed
Objectifies	Intense rage	Depression	Able to trust	Controlling	Hyper	Demanding
Bully/violence	Quarrelsome	Fear of loss	Tolerates ambivalence	Affect disconnected	Angry	Dehumanizing
Splits objects	Injury felt immediate	"mis-fit kid"	Sees alternatives	Disoriented		Infantile
High stress level	Join a gang	Substance abuse	Motivated	Tries to hold limelight		
Lack of soothing Mechanisms	Run away	Abuse self	Self-empathy	Feel like a fake		
	Easily seduced	Addictions	Good memory			

Explanation of Cathexis Scale

The middle of the scale, which is the optimal zone of cathexis, is when parents hold a child in mind and are consistent in response to the child. They are well attached to the child and maintain a state of good object constancy. The parent has a good volitional memory of who that child is and also a good mental representation of who that child could become in the future. In the present the parents are able to let the child determine who he or she "isn't," and these parents permit access to themselves so that the child always feels the parent is available.

These "good enough parents" are empathic and are able to tolerate ambivalence. They can accept when a child is angry with them as well as when the child is loving. These parents maintain good boundaries, knowing that the generation gap is a developmental necessity. They can say "no" and mean it and follow through. They have "eyes in the back of their head" because they know their child so well. There is an uninterrupted investment in the child that allows them to hold the child in mind even when the child is not present. They are parentally in love with the child.

As an example, one summer day I was talking to one of my neighbors while all the children were playing in the backyard. Suddenly this wonderfully cathected woman said to me, "Just a minute, Phil; I will be right back." She ran into the backyard and was gone for a few minutes and then came back to pick up the conversation where it left off. When I wondered why she had taken off into the backyard, she said that the kids were starting to fight in the backyard and she wanted to stop it before it got out of hand. I had heard nothing, not one sound, but this well-cathected parent picked up the slightest sound of change coming from the backyard and knew exactly what was going on and what she needed to do.

If the parents or the significant nurturant love objects have achieved this "good enough" cathexis, the child will be able to make friends because he or she can trust and have a good reciprocal interactional process with other people. The child will have reasonable good boundaries and will be able to seek comfort with significant adults when comfort is needed. The child will be able to tolerate opposing feelings (tolerate ambivalence) and also express real empathy to others and also himself or herself.

Self-empathy in childhood is often expressed in the ability to say no when the child feels something is either morally wrong or beyond his or her abilities or capabilities of following through. The child will be able to see alternatives and act on them and generally will be an intrinsically motivated student. These children will also be able to validate their own feelings, mainly because they have had their feelings validated by the significant love object. This optimal cathexis zone is really the best place for children to learn, because their brain arousal levels will be low and they will have the capacity to rest.

To the left of the continuum, toward decathexis, is "casual forgetting." (This may loosely coordinate with Main's insecure disorganized type of attachment.)[36] In casual forgetting, parents are often overcommitted and zealous toward their careers or occupations. Ruby Payne stated in one of her books, "To move from poverty to middle class or middle class to wealth, an individual must give up relationships for achievement (at least for some period of time)."[37] These high-achieving parents have the goal of "making it in life." They often propose that their cathexis is to their job and rationalize that it is actually helping the family for them to make a lot of money. This is a sad excuse for what becomes a casual forgetting or casual decathexis of their children.

On occasion this category also contains traumatized parents who themselves have suffered a measure of loss of significant love objects. This level of decathexis demonstrates clearly a preoccupied parent who must look directly at the child in order to truly hear the child. Even when the parent is with the child the parent may not really "be there," because his or her mind is somewhere else. On occasion these parents indulge in substance abuse, such as alcohol or "recreational drugs," and can often be unpredictable to the child. These parents should be a source of security but now are a source of fear because of the unpredictability. The child could approach the significant love object and not know whether he or she will be soothed, snapped at, or ignored.

Sometimes in this category parents are quite controlling in their care of the child, but it is to satisfy their own needs and not out of protection for the child. These parents tend to have an "evocative memory" of their child and bring their child into mind when they see an object that the child owns, as a trigger to picture their child. These parents would rarely muse over where their child is and what their child is doing from their volitional memory.

Children of these parents are usually quite obsessive with friends because they fear that the friend could be lost. In this category children have a slight depression and can be easily disoriented. Their confusion seems to come from their great investment in keeping people close and staying noticed and liked by others.

Sometimes children become a bit apathetic and become fearful very quickly. Children sometimes even "freeze" and become unable to move or function when their fears of loss become quickly accelerated.

Sometimes these kids are classified by their peers as misfits and can become the brunt of jokes. These kids are a little out of touch socially, mainly because they struggle with holding people in their mind. In that respect it is a reflection of the parental holding or lack thereof.

These children on occasion turn to substance abuse to medicate themselves and reduce their anxiety, and one of the greater "soothing" addictions is food. Sexual promiscuity is also an addiction, as well as shoplifting. Shoplifting is not so much a decision to accumulate objects as it is a continuous attempt to get something that is satisfying. Unfortunately the feeling of secure and consistent attachment is something that cannot be stolen. It is possible to steal objects, but it is not possible to steal a feeling.

Sometimes these kids are hoarders. I interviewed a young man who had forty boxes of cereal under his bed, not because his parents did not feed him, but because he was sometimes forgotten, and he tried to feel secure by stockpiling food underneath his bed.

Farther left on the continuum toward decathexis is intermittent decathexis. This parallels with Ainsworth's insecure ambivalence attachment. Parents who intermittently decathect their children often have low self-esteem themselves and need lots of self-reinforcement, called "narcissistic supplies." These parents tend to be poor cue readers, and the child could be emitting danger signals and the parent simply does not pick them up. Often these parents are themselves anxious or hostile and have been intermittently decathected in their own childhood by their own parents.

These parents will respond to their children if they provide narcissistic gratification or are an extension of themselves, like the "football dad" who fully owns his son and is cathected to him during the football season but is decathected when football ends. These parents treat the child as non-existent on an intermittent basis. This is an unconscious process; parents do not consciously tell themselves to intermittently decathect their child.

Intermittently decathexed children are clingy and avoidant at the same time. They want to interact with and attach to the parent but at the same time realize that it may be allowed for only a short period of time and therefore push away also.

There is intense rage at the significant love object, and these children are always in a high brain arousal state. These children tend to be quarrelsome and are difficult to comfort and soothe. I believe that in this particular category one will see the most domestic violence. The child becomes enraged at the parent and may physically fight or hurt the parent and vice versa.

These children immediately feel what is called narcissistic injury, meaning an injury to their sense of self and their sense of value. These children are often withdrawn from the family, and it is not unusual for kids in this category to run away or to join a gang in order to gain acceptance. This, however, is only an illusion, and the gang inevitably becomes unfulfilling as well.

I was treating one fourteen-year-old boy who was very intermittently decathexed and who had run away from home several times and was actually gone for weeks at a time. The family looked for the child, and when the child finally came home the reunion was a time of intense cathexis, followed by decathexis because of the parents' work schedule. When I asked this young man why he ran away from home, he said it was to protect his parents; if he had not run away from home his own rage would have caused him to attack his parents physically, and he did not want to do that. His running away from home was actually an attempt to save his parents as well as an attempt to draw attention to himself and beg his parents to come look for him. He was able to attain two goals by one act.

The children in this category have such a tremendous need to be loved consistently that they are easily seduced by the wrong people, whether it be gangs or pedophiles. These young people present vulnerability because of their overwhelming need for closeness. These kids also seem to present as prime sexual abuse victims for adults on the lookout for just such intermittently decathected young people.

The last category, which is severe deprivation or total decathexis, correlates loosely with Ainsworth's insecure avoidance type of attachment. In this category the parents are, for many reasons of their own, unable to sustain a whole object relationship and a secure attachment to the child. These children feel that they get nothing from their parents, because the eyes of their parents are never positive mirrors for any of their performance. These parents tend to not see the child as real, as valuable, or as special in their own right. Sometimes the parents are actually physically abusive or neglectful; however, they do not see themselves as decathexing parents because often they reflect what they have grown up with in their own family of origin.

When I interview a decathected parent I find that they really do not know their child, such as specific likes and dislikes, who the child hangs out with, or what the child may be doing on any given day. They treat the child as someone who is an "unknown"; therefore they have very little to report. There is very little sustaining memory of the child, and this parent can walk away from the family and leave the children with grandparents or with another parent. Seriously decathected parents could walk past their children in a department store and literally not recognize them. The child would have to call out "Dad" or "Mom" in order for the decathected parent to recognize the child. As unbelievable as this sounds, I am seeing more and more of this type of decathexis in families.

Severely deprived and decathected children have very weak and porous consciences. They actively ignore adults, particularly their parents, and people in general tend to be more like objects than real. They have difficulty empathizing, but they can put on a great front, like a classic "used car salesman," when they want to get whatever they feel they need. They often express violence toward others and can be bullies, especially if their own desires are blocked. They rarely express anxiety, because to do so would bring on more rejection from their families; therefore they've learned to shut down the expression of anxiety, even though it is still below the surface.

These kids tend to see people as either all good or all bad, and that is subject to change at a moment's notice depending on whether or not the adults are giving the kids what they want. There is usually a high level of stress in these children, and they travel in Dr. Perry's state of brain alarm on a continual basis. They tend to be orderly to the point of being rigid and compulsive.

Because of the deprivation that these children suffer, Dr. Perry might call them "brain damaged." These children have lost a love object, and they also have lost the object's assistance in modulating and countering inner aggressive forces. Attachment is all about security and outside safety as well as inside safety. When adults are not there to help children soothe and learn how to temper impulses and aggression, the aggression reigns.

In *Lost Boys: Why Our Sons Turn Violent and How We Can Help Them,* James Garbarino interviewed adolescents who were in jail for murder. An adult prisoner made a chilling statement to Garbarino's colleague: "I'd rather be wanted for murder than not wanted at all."[38]

These decathected children do not tend to hurt members of their own families but are violent toward members of society that are no relation to them. These children are not beyond help, but this particular category is growing in numbers.

The first category to the right of center on the cathexis scale is the first degree of hyper-cathexis: the parent who is very involved and does everything with his or her child. The child is more like a "buddy" than a child who is autonomous and separate. These parents tend to be boundary violators and want to partake in many of the child's functions, even peer functions. The parent subtly gives the child the message "Be what I want you to be and fulfill the picture for your life that I picture in my head."

These parents tend to be somewhat unpredictable and spontaneous, which to some degree comes off as fun for the child. These parents also tend to be perfectionistic but on occasion lose their sense of separateness and forget that they and their child are two separate individuals. These parents tend to be somewhat controlling, not allowing the child to take too many risks and even asking the child to follow a verbal script of things to say in various circumstances. The casual observer might think that this is a good parent, although slightly over-involved with the child. Upon further investigation and scrutiny one can see that the boundaries between the child and the adult are blurred.

With a hyper-cathected parent, the children tend to be over-achievers but often report feeling "fake." They really do not feel comfortable being on their own. These children tend to be somewhat apprehensive and a bit controlling in their own right, and they express feelings that are somewhat stilted and robotic. These children try to hold the limelight, knowing this will please the parent, but they are easily upset and even disoriented when this is not possible. Children in this category really love their parents a great deal and want them to be around but feel stifled in spontaneous action or internal feelings.

The next category right of center is second-degree hyper-cathexis, and it amounts to parents doing more "for" the child than "with" them. Parents tend to be more intrusive as well as more indulgent and give the child pretty much what the child wants. The parents often give child lots of money, quickly come to the aid of the child when he or she gets into trouble, completely take the child's side, and argue, advocate, and pay the price for the child's consequences. The child pays the emotional price of not being able to establish a separate identity or autonomy.

These parents have a difficult time saying no and constantly worry that the child may not love them. They get quite a bit of pleasure out of children who "act like them," which tends at least unconsciously to cut off a sense of autonomous mastery in the child. The parent often describes the child as "good" if the child acquiesces to be part of the parent. When the parents mirror the child's achievements they are really mirroring themselves and are not sensitive to the individual separate signals of the child. Any anxiety in the child brings out hostility in the parent and a puzzled sense of how the child could be so anxious when the child is so well cared for.

Children in the second degree of hyper-cathexis feel angry much of the time over feelings of incompetence and constantly having to mirror the parents' performance. Children may verbalize that they feel like they are living their parents' lives. The children also have a difficult time saying no and struggle with basic self-esteem in terms of their own capabilities, skills, and achievements.

There is often a love-hate relationship with the parent; the child loves the parents for what they do *for* the child but hates them for what they do *to* the child. Sometimes these children do outrageous things, such as sneaking into the school principal's office after hours and depositing feces on top of the principal's desk. This risk-taking behavior is also attention getting and a statement of anger over an attempt to establish identity, separateness, and power.

The third degree hyper-cathexis category, anxious preoccupation, is the most extreme form of the parent living out the child's life. The child is viewed by the parent as "other me" or the "younger me," and the parent has obsessive thoughts about how the child is growing and obsessive fears about whether the child will leave, die, or be kidnapped. A parent in this category would never consider taking a vacation without the child because there really is no separate child. The parent really attempts to become the sole soothing mechanism for the child, both internally and externally. This is a complete denial of the child's separateness and autonomous function.

In many cases the parents does not seem to be able to bear the thought of the child growing or maturing, because maturation may indicate separation. When the child makes separate movements, the parent may lash out with hostility and in some cases severely deprive the child to teach the child a lesson. The parent often sees danger to the child to the point of homeschooling the child and filtering every outside contact. This hyper-cathexis process actually is a paradoxical form of decathexis of a separate identity. Over-involvement of this magnitude is a decathexis of the child as a separate person.

The child's response to this type of omnipresent parenting is to vacillate between not taking any risks at all and being a dangerous risk taker and even a self-mutilator. The self-mutilation may come from a child who is actually trying to feel something on his or her own, apart from what the parent tells the child to feel. These children tend to not learn to soothe themselves or control their internal state, because everything is controlled for them. They tend to be total perfectionists and are subject to extreme temper tantrums or actual rage reactions.

The child feels tremendously dehumanized and turns around and dehumanizes peers in much the same way. Children express, when honest, that they are really not living life but playing a role. These children are often self-absorbed and extremely demanding and never expect to feel any pain, because the parents usually run interference for them. If these children should happen to feel pain, they cry foul and see the world as a depriving, rejecting place within which to live.

They also tend to split people into all good and all bad objects, depending on how they are treated. Relationships tend to be extremely infantile and immature, based on getting what they want. These children are often mean to others and can exhibit sudden vicious violence with almost the same intensity as the completely decathexed child at the opposite end of this continuum. One youngster said, "I often feel like a vampire getting his picture taken. You know vampires eat, drink, talk, wear clothes, and all the other stuff, but when the picture develops they don't exist; they're invisible, and when I look into a mirror I see no image."

It is possible to damage a child emotionally by decathecting him or her and having little or no relationship with the child or by establishing such a smothering hyper-cathexis that the child feels like a non-entity. It is not good for a child not to be loved, but is also not good for a child to be obsessively loved. It is possible to severely reject a child on both ends of the continuum. The results look frighteningly similar: rage!

CHAPTER 15

Decathexis and Corrective Measures

Today's school classrooms are really the primary mental health facilities for our children. Even though this chapter with its corrective measures is intended for the classroom, it is absolutely applicable to any other caregiving setting or home. Many of the corrective measures are similar or identical to the corrective measures mentioned in the chapter on psychological trauma. When that happens, the corrective measure will be stated but not explained.

The first effect of decathexis is that the child has a difficult time forming an integrated positive body image. These children do not protect themselves well, tend to be heedless, and often engage in dangerous risk-taking activities. These children have a general dislike for who they are anatomically, socially, and emotionally.

It is important to encourage same-sex mentors: grandmas and grandpas, coaches, teachers, club leaders, and good neighbors. Every boy and every girl needs a same-sex mentor to stand in awe of the child and mirror the child's accomplishments.

Another corrective measure is to attend to every ache and pain that the child has. The more you attend to children when they are in need, the more they will manage with less of you.

It is very helpful to put children's pictures up in the classroom. I was called to consult on a disruptive first grader who was hurting kids and was really out of control in the classroom. I noticed during lunch that the young man in question was extremely artistic with his food. He did not eat a lot of food; he would make structures, castles, and various sculptures from the plate of vegetables and fruit that he had. At the end of the day I asked the primary teachers where they saw this child twenty years from today. The unanimous response was prison. The mental picture they had of this child was that he would end up seriously hurting someone.

I told the teachers that it was a major problem when they had this kind of future mental representation of this child. I then mentioned the child's fascination with creating sculptures out of food. The teachers agreed that he loved to play with his food and was often quite artistic.

I suggested that twenty years from today all of the people at that consultation would be paying this young man thirty dollars a plate to eat in his restaurant. I suggested that in the future they call him "the chef," not to his face but only while they were conferencing about him. We also went over other behavioral techniques to use with this young man, not the least of which was a lot of protection and nurturance.

I checked back six weeks later and was pleased and amazed to hear the reports that "the chef" had made a 180-degree behavioral turn and was now performing better in class and significantly better academically. All of the teachers and administrators were visualizing this young man as a famous restaurant chef. Not one person relayed this verbally to the child, but the change in the mental representation and the expectation was such that this child picked up a positive picture from the classroom and school personnel.

The teachers also took me up on the suggestion that they take pictures of each of the classroom children and put the pictures up on the board next to a cut-out magazine picture representing who each child could become in fifteen to twenty years. Beside this problem child's picture was an exquisite picture of a chef smiling from ear to ear, looking as if he had created the Taj Mahal out of the plate of food.

Additional corrective measures include using the child's name a lot and valuing that name in classroom conversations. PE books are essential for children like this and help the child get a mental image of a person who has skills, accomplishments, and values. Students with poor self-image tend to blame themselves for every failure, and then when they have successes they attribute those successes to external factors such as fate. The child's sense of attribution is skewed, and he or she rarely attributes success to hard work or personal perseverance. This is where the teacher's mental representation comes in and can help the student personalize his or her accomplishments.

When these children put themselves down with negative comments such as "I'm stupid" or "I'm ugly," immediately require the student to change his or her physical state. It is important for decathected children to move and physically act their way into feeling better. This erases those verbal interjects that are negative in nature and heard from inside.

Another corrective measure for body image is to have adults who have the capacity to nurture touch the child as much as possible. Unfortunately in many school systems there are rules against teachers touching students for fear of sexual abuse or charges being brought up against the school administration. The decathected child is extremely touch hungry, so an appropriate touch, such as a pat on the back, a high-five, or a handshake, certainly qualifies as good touch.

On occasion it is appropriate for teachers to allow students to lean against them during reading time or activity times as long as it is done appropriately. Leaning against a nurturing adult is extremely satisfying for a touch-hungry decathected child, but don't scare the child by asking the child to admit the feeling of warmth.

The second effect that occurs in a decathected child is tremendously low self-esteem: the feeling of "I'm nothing." These children may rip up their art projects or not hand in homework after they've done it. These easily frustrated children see only one solution to a problem. They assume very quickly that others hate them.

The corrective measure for helping children with low self-esteem is first of all to listen. Listening to a child with your whole mind and body is extremely therapeutic and extremely underrated. Part of listening is being empathic. Oftentimes children do not need answers but simply an acknowledgement that they are being understood.

A decathected child will often say "Nothing ever goes right for me" or "I never get to do anything." Everything is put into extremes, so ask questions that challenge that "always-never" thinking. The decathected child often will say "I'm no good." Ask the child if that voice came from the inside or from somebody on the outside. If kids can differentiate the introjected voices from the outside voices, they know which voice to combat and are better able to do so by changing their physical states.

Additional corrective measures for low self-esteem include the use of appreciative praise, trying to hold eye contact, and being the perfect mirror. Give decathected children permission to ask for help. Children who think they are nothing don't believe they can ask other people for help. Tell them that it is okay and that they should ask for help.

Getting to know a decathected child is also extremely important in the process of forming an attachment. To help the child become human and real is a goal that will pay off behaviorally as well as academically. Most people do not understand the tremendous narcissistic injury that these children have that contributes to their low self-image. It is a narcissistic injury when a parent cannot or does not love the child as much as he or she needs to be loved. It is also a narcissistic injury when the child cannot make the parent love the child enough, and this affects body integrity and sense of self and esteem and produces tremendous rage and a potential for violence.

A third result of decathected children is that they end up being hurtful to any kind of considerate relationship. They push people away and cannot tolerate both good and angry feelings toward one person at the same time. They desperately want intimacy but ward people off as much as possible. Their theme statements are "I hate you; please don't leave me" or "Go away closer." An unexpected luxury for such a child is a loving person who can be safely hated and who won't leave the child.

Corrective measures for this kind of behavior include consistently pointing out to the child that anger is a temporary state and that the child will again like the adult later on. It is important to predict the trauma cycle of friendship (see page 145) and also important to teach accurate cue reading. The detached and decathected child has a difficult time reading faces or actions and often misreads them as aggressive and hateful. Encourage decathected kids to ask and do active reality testing when they see someone's face in a scowl.

Adults can talk descriptively about the countenance of others. A teacher could say, "Oh, look, he's smiling at you. I think he wants to play." Have kids practice facial expressions in front of a mirror. Not only do children need to become good at reading other people's cues, they also need to read their own "signal anxiety" cues and thus gain an important feedback loop to monitor their own behavior.

An eighteen-year-old who is in therapy because of a lifetime of feeling detached is a very poor cue reader. After seeing him for some time and teaching him how to read cues, I still occasionally get a call on the telephone when he is puzzled by what other people mean when they say certain things or what their body language is trying to say. He still checks out reality with me on occasion, and after he is satisfied that he has learned additional cues and the meaning of them, he continues a positive progression toward good socialization.

The next consequence of decathexis is the inability of the child to master physical separation or hold mental pictures of loving people. In addition to the corrective measures mentioned in the chapter on psychological trauma, it is sometimes helpful for these kids to play memory games. Memory games seem to help children connect the pictures and talk and formulate a good mental image inside of their heads that they can volitionally call up when they want to.

It is also important for them to call up a mental picture of themselves being successful. When functioning on their own or even being alone, they need to have safe images inside of their heads. The greatest intrinsic motivation of any child comes from his or her own perceived competence. To have perceived competence, one must hold a good picture of one's self inside one's head.

The fifth consequence and effect of decathexis upon a child is that it sets the child up for maltreatment. Sexual predators and perpetrators love to prey upon the decathected child. These children accept abusive behavior because it is better than nothing; in fact, they expect it as part of who they are. These children also demonstrate a lack of feeling and deny pain, usually shutting off all of their emotions, which again makes them prime victims for perpetrators. These children are often searching desperately to find a nurturant person to protect the illusion of a loving parent and therefore will accept all kinds of hurtful behavior to perpetuate that illusion.

Corrective measures include talking to the child about safety and telling the child that there are two people that children need protection from: "others" and "themselves." Decathected children provoke others to reject them and start that trauma cycle of relationships. They therefore need protection from themselves and from their own provocative behavior.

Decathected children have a terrible time trying to keep themselves safe, either because of the provocative behavior or because they are daredevils and take risks. They also isolate affect and sometimes don't even realize that they are being hurt.

A seventeen-year-old boy told me that the night before he had a really great time because it was so exciting: he drove at midnight from Grand Rapids, Michigan, to Kalamazoo, Michigan (a distance of about 35 miles) at 110 miles an hour the entire way. When I said that this was extremely dangerous risk-taking behavior, he remarked, "You haven't heard the best part yet. I drove the whole distance with no lights on." This youngster was certainly setting himself up for great bodily harm and even death because of his lack of concern for his own self and safety and also showed no concern for the safety or welfare of other people.

As a corrective measure, if possible, do not allow decathected children to isolate themselves. Remember, especially for these children, the opposite of love is "nothing." If these kids want to sit by themselves or work by themselves, try to find a safe and acceptable person to sit by them and help them. Emphasize and show these children how they are accepted and where they belong. Belonging and feeling a part of a larger community is therapeutic for the decathected child.

Make sure that the children's feelings get acknowledged, and work to label what their feelings are. Children need to not only recognize but also label a feeling in order to feel a sense of mastery or control over it. Validate children's feelings, particularly if the feeling is fear. Define fear for the child as nature's protection and suggest to the really tough children that courage is not an absence of fear but the ability to continue to put one foot ahead of the other and progress in a positive manner toward a goal, even when afraid.

Another consequence of decathexis is that the decathected child has poor impulse control. The normal goal of anger is to solve the problem of how to be close to someone. This is not the case with a decathected child, who uses anger and lack of impulse control as a soothing mechanism or a survival tactic. During decathexis the child feels so alone that he or she is overwhelmed by impulses and drives and has no mentor or parent to modulate his or her feelings and provide a sense of control. Rage therefore is a soothing mechanism because is represents self-empathy to the decathected child. It also represents at least a temporary relief from tension, which may be why many decathected children listen to outrageous and vicious singing groups chanting murder, mayhem, and total disrespect for authority. An adolescent once told me, "If all parents knew how to love their children, there would be no vicious rock bands spouting obscenities and mayhem the way there are today. Kids would not need these groups to express the rage they feel."

In general the best way to deal with impulse control of a decathected child is to assure them of three things: safety, structure and routine, and a person to attach to. The most reliable way to ratchet up aggression in a decathected child is to isolate the child. Isolation for the decathected child is to encourage delusions of grandeur and feelings of omnipotence. Isolation also seems to increase the reactivity level to the behavior of other people and increased startle responses due to lack of experience predicting other people's movements.

If the teacher needs to give the child a timeout in a separate room, the child should never be alone. A significant nurturing adult needs to accompany this child. I have had numerous children tell me that they have a "dragon on the inside" and that when they get angry the dragon comes out and gets loose. A child isolated in a separate room is in the room with the loose wild dragon. The child may rip the room to shreds and break as many things as possible to ward off the feeling of being killed by his own dragon.

When a safe, nurturing adult goes into a timeout room, allow the child to spout off and talk about how angry he or she is.

Once the youngster starts to calm down, a simple routine of asking four questions can be helpful. The first question is "What did you do?" Children need to be able to describe and label exactly what it is that they did that was inappropriate.

The next question is "When you did that, what did you want?" Kids usually name something tangible, but if pushed a little further they may come up with something intangible, such as a feeling of being liked.

The next request: "List four other things that you could have done other than to act out." Sometimes children come up with ingenious activities or ideas, many of which would be permissible in the future.

The last question is "What will you do next time this comes up?" Give the child the idea that the difficulties will in fact come up again and the child will be called upon to control impulses and figure out an appropriate way of handling the feelings on the inside. He or she needs to be able to "tame the dragon."

It is helpful to talk to kids about safe ways to be angry. These might include talking with another person, writing a letter, drawing a picture, or physically jogging or running. (I do not recommend punching or kicking as a physical outlet, even if it is against an inanimate object.) Role-playing and performing skits are helpful ways to express anger and channel impulses. Teach kids to use as many soothing mechanisms as possible.

A seventh consequence of decathexis is the lack of boundary formation. When teaching boundaries to children it is extremely important that teachers have good, solid boundaries of their own. Follow through is an absolute must, and all of the boundaries, such as body boundaries, emotional boundaries, mental boundaries, verbal boundaries, and space boundaries, need to be guarded in both the child and the teacher as an essential component of helping the child.

The last consequence of decathexis is that the decathected child, if left untreated, becomes a decathecting adult. Detachment, rejection, and decathexis are not things that children can climb out of on their own. In order to learn how to attach, the child needs to get pulled out of decathexis and out of this method of interacting with people.

Attachment is transferable: knowing how to attach in a loving, nurturing manner to at least one person allows for the transfer of that capacity and ability onto new people. Unfortunately, the opposite is also true. If a child grows up decathexed and unattached, not knowing how to develop a capacity for a good relationship, that lack of ability also gets passed on to new people. Relationships then become a process of using each other in an instrumental fashion rather than genuine reciprocal pleasure and giving of self.

The ultimate corrective measure, therefore, is to keep the child from becoming a decathected adult. By being consistently provided with nurturance, predictability, firm rules, and a loving picture inside, this human being will feel valuable and will develop to his or her full potential.

CHAPTER 16

Child Assessment

This chapter is intended for the schoolteacher, but it is applicable for anyone who wants to assess the etiology of a child's behavior. Without looking at the context of the child's experience, any intervention will be misdirected, while a complete assessment will automatically lead to specific interventions.

There are eight main areas to examine for an accurate assessment of what's going on within the child.

1. Demographics: This includes information such as the name of the child, the age of the child, the sex, the race, and the cultural context. Sometimes demographics are extremely informative, even something simple like a child's name. I often ask whether the child has a pet name or a nickname. Nicknames or pet names can tell a great deal about the contexts within which the child lives and can be helpful in adjusting the child's sense of self and identity. Age also is important because older children should have better impulse control, more abstract brain function, better speech and language, and a more advanced use of logical consequences.

Race and culture are also extremely important. I was called to examine a child because he had round red welts all over his back. The teacher thought that the child was being physically abused, and I suggested that protective services be contacted, as well as the parent. Through an interpreter, the child's mother explained that the child had some respiratory illness and that in Vietnam respiratory illness was treated by putting hot stones on the person's back to draw out the infection and clear the lungs. It was evident that this was not a case of abuse but a well-intended use of homeopathy. Cultural issues may enter in and certainly influence the diagnostic assessment.

2. Background information: A good assessment requires information about the family constellation, the child's medical history, and the known strengths and special abilities of the child. Any history of anyone in the family experiencing trauma is also helpful, because if a sibling or parent has suffered life-threatening illness, the kinds of fears that often get expressed in children could be explained rather readily. Background and family information allows for the determination of the number of "safe people" available to the child who can function as protectors or support systems.

3. Specific concerns. What behaviors make the child a candidate for assessment? Often that child who exhibits the traits that the teacher finds most difficult to handle is the child who is assessed first. In other words, a teacher who personally fears aggression will want aggressive children assessed first. In talking about concerns, be specific and list the antecedents to the behavior as well as the specific behavior itself. It is also helpful to cover the types of interventions already being used by the teacher and whether or not these interventions have been helpful.

4. Speech and language skills: Does the child have good expressive and receptive speech and language? Can the child express himself or herself articulately and clearly, and does the child understand what people are saying? Is the child able to follow directions, maintain eye contact, use gestures, and identify or know the functions of things? Can the child produce clear sounds and word combinations? Can the child establish a reciprocal conversation where questions might be asked and answered so that there is a back and forth interaction?

A child who speaks well tends to be less physically aggressive. Words actually give a child a sense of power, and therefore articulate children can establish a significant sense of power with their words rather than with their fists.

5. Motor skills: Does the child have fine motor skills? Can he or she grasp a pencil? Is there eye-hand coordination so the child can

produce something recognizable on paper? Also look at balance and posture and whether or not the child has freedom of movement. Children who are struggling with some sensory integration dysfunctions will use motor skills to integrate their words and information coming into the brain. In other words, these children will often need to be moving some part of their body in order to comprehend, understand, and interact.

The last three assessment areas are the major areas of functioning within a social context.

6. Relationships: How does the child approach peers and adults? Is there a balance with talking to peers and adults? Or does the child want to interact and play with only one age group of people? Does the child have friends? How many, what type, and how old are they? Does the child play with others cooperatively, in a parallel fashion, or not at all? One of the big issues is whether the child can trust other people. This is assessed by watching the proximity that the child has with others, whether or not there is touch going on, and whether or not there is eye contact or speech usage.

Another question is whether the child needs everyone in the environment to be consistent. All children need consistency and predictability—a sense of routine—to some extent. But some children need such predictability that if there is not absolute predictability and consistency, the child will freak out. Does the child demonstrate separation problems or fear loss of people? This will tell a great deal about the child's ability to maintain consistent internal objects. Can the child be angry with a peer and still stay friends with that child? This assesses the child's capacity to tolerate ambivalence and can indicate to what level the child has progressed. Is the child capable of feeling real empathy? Real empathy does not get expressed by a child who has not been empathized with.

Is the child respectful of personal boundaries, or is the child a boundary violator? A boundary-violating child who feels free to trespass at-will is usually a child who lives in an environment where the boundaries are very fluid or nonexistent. Do people seem to be real objects to the child or simply instruments to be used? Can the child make real attachments with friends in the classroom, and does this child know other children's names? The aggressive child has such a difficult time attaching and relating that he or she generally only knows one or two children's names, and therefore it becomes very easy to objectify other children and then hurt them. The more real the child makes the other children in the classroom, the less of an ability the child will have to hurt others physically. Acting out children should learn the children's names and establish relationships, which will dramatically reduce any violent, aggressive acting out or hurtful behavior.

7. Cognitive functioning and thought process: Is the child able to solve problems and see solutions, or does the child panic quickly and become unable to think sequentially? Is the child goal directed and able to picture success in his or her mind and attempt to achieve something that he or she can visualize? Many children do not see a future or even short-term goals, because their energy is taken up in surviving today.

Does the child worry about the same topic over and over again? The child may express themes in play such as people leaving or people getting beat up or hurt and continue to express these over and over again. Does the child express any fantasies or verbalize any possible fears? Does the child consciously identify with mentors or adults of the same sex? Does the child express any fears of bodily injury?

Can the child remember simple tasks or yesterday's good experiences? Traumatized children have a memory that only seems to remember bad or dangerous things that happened. They remember few positive interactions or good things that went on in their environment. Can the child recognize his or her achievements? Can the child monitor personal behavior in relation to responses from other children in a group? This indicates that the child has a good "observing ego" and is able to self-monitor. I would not expect a fully intact observing ego until about the age of six or seven in most children.

Can the child make logical consequence connections and follow a two-step plan? Can the child tie his or her behavior to other people's responses and also engage in reality testing to determine whether people are talking about him or her or what exactly the meaning of a conversation is? It's important to know if the child can read cues accurately and if the child is oriented to time, place, and person. A traumatized child who lives in a dangerous environment may need to be oriented so that aggressive defensive skills do not kick in.

8. Coping skills and coping style (defense mechanisms): Are people afraid of this child, and is the child afraid of himself or herself? Children will sometimes warn adults that they are going to lose control, a signal that the child has a fear of himself or herself and knows that he or she has an inability to control impulses. Isolation is another defense mechanism to identify.

Is the child constantly on the move in the classroom? What is the child's activity level and the child's attention span? Children who feel unsafe often regress to an earlier age of behavior and will engage in whining or screaming, both of which link to trust factors.

Does the child become attacking or identify with aggressive individuals? Does the child need absolute control? This child often sits by the door, does not play in a crowd, wears his or her coat, does not use the toilet at school, gets to school early or not at all, and plays with much younger children or alone. These are indications that the child views life as a bit scary and must maintain absolute control.

Is the child counter phobic: really fearful but denies the fear by being a daredevil? A counter phobic child is so afraid that history will repeat itself that he or she wants to demonstrate absolute control over whether the danger would prevail. This becomes a coping mechanism to deal with a constant level of anxiety regarding danger.

Look at passive-aggressive tactics; sometimes youngsters drive teachers up the wall by being skilled procrastinators or suddenly developing a "hearing problem." It is almost impossible to deal with a passive-aggressive child without first turning the passivity into active, overt aggression and then dealing with the overt aggression in logical-consequence ways.

How many soothing mechanisms does the child use? Does the child have more than one way to cope with anxiety and fear, and does the child use more sophisticated coping skills or the primitive hitting or denial methods of coping?

Teachers should ask "What feeling does the child elicit in me?" Oftentimes the teacher's feelings about the child are key in understanding what the child thinks and fears most. It is not unusual to find a child who has fear of death or of being hurt, and the feeling that is elicited in the teacher is fear that the child is going to hurt himself or herself through heedless actions. The elicited feelings in the teacher therefore are usually correlated very closely with the actual intention and feelings of the child.

When I observe a child I generally use a sheet like figure 6. Sometimes I fill it in through observation, or I ask the teacher to fill it in so that we can discuss the teacher's responses and formulate a classroom treatment plan.

Figure 6 (see next page)

Case Study Worksheet

Child's Name:	Date:
Team Members:	

SPEECH AND LANGUAGE:	**RELATIONSHIPS TO PEOPLE:**

Expressive:
  • Any sound
  • Combinations
 	
Receptive:
  • Eye Contact
  • Imitates gestures
  • Follows directions
  • Identifies
  • Knows functions	

MOTOR:
 	
Fine Motor:
  • Grasp
  • Eye/hand coordination
 	
Gross Motor:
  • Body movement
  • Balance
  • Posture
 	
Neurological/Physical impairment?
	COGNITIVE FUNCTIONING AND THOUGH PROCESS:

GENERAL IMPRESSIONS:
 	
  • Observable feelings in child
 	
  • Feelings child elicits in others
 	
  • Attention span
 	
  • Activity level
 	
SUPPORT SYSTEMS:
	COPING STYLE RELATED TO STRESS AND ANXIETY:

To determine whether a child should be referred to special services or for a psychological-social emotional assessment, figure 7 outlines a simple rating scale that can produce points. Depending on the number of points the child has, the teacher could then judge whether to refer the child to a child development specialist, a school social worker, or a psychologist. This child assessment level system scale (CALS) covers physical difficulties, speech and language difficulties, and motor difficulties, the thought process relationships and coping styles of the child, and whether the child has an emotional support system. With this scale teachers can assign points to each area and quickly assess whether a child should be referred for additional observation and special services. This scale is by no means scientific, but it can provide teachers with an easy method of knowing whether to call in help for a specific child.

Figure 7 (see next page)

Child Assessment Level System (CALS)

Formulated by Phillip D. Hamberg ©

AREA	1 POINT	2 POINTS	3 POINTS	4 POINTS	TOTAL POINTS
PHYSICAL PROBLEMS	Minor physical problems (something correctable)	Has one significant physical problem	Has two significant physical problems	Has more than three significant problems	
SPEECH & LANGUAGE	Low to almost average range of expressive and receptive language	Mild deficit in expressive or receptive language	Significant deficit in expressive or receptive language	Significant deficit in both receptive and expressive language	
MOTOR MOVEMENT	Low to almost average range of fine and gross motor movement	Mild deficit in fine or gross motor movement	Significant deficit in fine or gross motor movement	Significant deficit in both fine and gross motor movement	
THOUGHT PROCESS	Low ability: 1. Solve problems 2. Plan ahead 3. Make decisions 4. Remember 5. Recognize logical consequences	Significant deficit in at least one of the five processes	Significant deficit in at least three of the five processes	Significant deficit in four or more thought processes	
RELATIONSHIPS	Limited ability to form friendly ties with peers and maintain them over time	Limited ability to form friendly ties with adults and maintain them over time	Isolates self/passive in warding off people in general	Active warding off of people (attaching) (Fearful to attach)	
COPING STYLE	Has at least four identifiable adaptive ways to cope with stress	Has at least two identifiable adaptive ways to cope with stress	Has one identifiable way to cope with stress	Has no identifiable ways to cope with stress that are adaptive	
SUPPORT SYSTEM	Has at least two observable significant supportive adults	Child has at least one adult and one older sibling as significant support people	Child has at least one observable supportive adult of any type	Child has no observable significant supportive adult	

9 points or less ----------- Monitor child's performance
10 – 16 points or less ----------- May need some specific special service
17 points or less ----------- Refer to Child Development Specialist

CHAPTER 17

The Dirty Dozen

This final chapter is for parents. This chapter is also applicable within the classroom setting and may also provide insight for teachers on how to interact with parents.

There are at least twelve issues that trip parents up in their childrearing role, and many of these "dirty dozen" have to do with erroneous assumptions that parents make about childrearing.

The first erroneous assumption is that parents can vaccinate their children against traumatic events by giving them trauma. Well-meaning parents will sometimes make their children walk home in the dark if they are afraid of the dark, presenting a childrearing pattern that is intended to build resiliency by forcing children to do things that they are terrified of doing. Giving a child purposely traumatic events to endure will not build up any kind of resiliency but will only prove that the parent is unwilling or unable to protect the child.

It is possible to vaccinate a child against trauma, but it is done by a consistent childrearing pattern where the parents are available and protective and absolutely predictable. Developing a safe mental picture of who the parent is on the inside and what the parent is willing to do for the child is really the vaccination. One vaccinates a child by teaching soothing mechanisms and helping the child to see where he or she has some kind of control. When a parent exploits the subjective state of helplessness of a child by giving more trauma, it only reinforces a belief that this world is an unsafe place within which to live.

The second erroneous assumption is that parents can hide major emotional issues from children. Attempting to hide issues such as death, severe illness, substance abuse, or an adversarial relationship with a close relative or spouse does not work, and children believe that the parents in attempting to do so are trying to deceive them.

Dealing with each issue at a developmental level appropriate to the child and answering questions simply and factually builds resiliency. If Mom and Dad are getting a divorce, it is much more therapeutic to tell children outright and then to emphasize that it is a "big people" problem and that the children had nothing to do with it and have no responsibility for the impending divorce. The facts and the plain truth will suffice.

The younger the child is, the more the child depends upon non-verbal cues, because they are much more accurate in predicting the intent of a parent. Children watch what the body says, what the eyes say, what the tone of voice says, and even the fluidity of movement. As the old expression goes, you can fool a fool, con a con, but you can't kid a kid.

The third erroneous assumption is that discipline means "to punish." *Discipline,* however, comes from a Latin word that means "to teach" and "to protect." Whenever a parent disciplines a child, it should be geared toward teaching the child appropriate options in terms of behavior. To physically punish, hurt, or inflict pain on a child simply teaches the child to stay away from the punisher.

One of the most important things a parent can do for a child is to discipline a child—asking the child to examine what the child did, what the child wanted, what the child could have done differently, and what the child will do next time—along with reparations that the child has to make as part of the logical consequences. When a parent does not discipline a child, the child inevitably thinks one of four things: My parent does not love me, my parents are scared of their own anger, my parents are scared of my anger, or my parents are afraid that I will hate them. Not to discipline puts the child in the parental role and in a position of omnipotence, a role most children will exploit, and a role that will damage the development of the child.

Another defeating assumption sometimes held by parents is that the child should approve of the parents, and parents should not make their children angry. This is a real boundary issue and a generation gap issue. Parents need to be consistent and involved with children and hold their children in their minds, but attempting to appear "cool" to the kids and relate on their level as a peer is ineffective and often downright silly. Children need cathexis and attachment, which tells the child that he or she is loved and accepted.

It is also perfectly okay if parents are angry with children and children are angry with parents. Resiliency in childhood means learning how to tolerate ambivalence. Children need to know that they can feel two different kinds of feelings toward the same person at the same time. They also need to know that love is not canceled if someone gets angry.

It should be noted that a well-attached child is attached for life and that this emotional attachment is next to impossible to break. Parents need to take comfort in a well-established relationship.

The fifth erroneous assumption that parents sometime have is that children should not own strong feelings. It is not unusual to hear a child scream that he or she hates someone and wishes that person were dead or to say flippantly, "I'll kill you." While the language should be discouraged, it is absolutely essential for the parents to validate feelings.

The validation takes the form of rephrasing the words to something like "You are really angry and even want to hurt someone right now." The validation is not giving permission to act on those feelings but a validation that the child *has* them. When a child's feelings are validated, it reinforces a system of security and safety within the child because the child starts to believe that feelings are valid and that the child is able to say "no" when he or she encounters people that do not have the child's best interest at heart.

The sixth erroneous assumption is that bad behavior is just "acting out" and a bid for attention. While it may be true, more often than not acting out is a way of communicating when the child doesn't know which words to use. It is essential to look past the behavior and find out what the child is really reacting to and trying to say. When the parent takes the attitudinal approach of "Your behavior is talking to me, and I'm trying to hear what it is saying," the child is helped to observe himself or herself and start to conceptualize the ability to articulate what it is he or she feels and how to go about getting that feeling met appropriately. The traumatized child is a perfect example, because children who have been traumatized lose their ability to watch and monitor themselves and live in a survival mode, which looks like constant acting out rather than attempting to communicate.

The seventh erroneous assumption states that it does not matter how you treat a very young child, because he or she will forget about it later on. Dr. Bruce Perry, a noted psychiatrist and researcher on brain function, researched neuro-response sensitization, which indicated that the brain can become sensitized very early in life and, once sensitized, is capable of remembering very early memories.[39] Not only does the brain remember but the body also seems to remember everything, particularly when it comes to trauma.

A kindergarten-age girl was referred to me for treatment because she was chasing children down on the playground, jumping on them, and then wrapping her hands around their throats and choking them. The little girl was not able to articulate why she was doing this other than the fact that she was very angry. An in-depth developmental history with this child's mother uncovered that about the time this girl was beginning to walk (nine months) the mother had a boyfriend who would discipline the little girl by choking her almost to unconsciousness. This went on until this mother threw this boyfriend out when the little girl was about fourteen months. The girl was never choked again, but when she got to an age where she could recognize her own anger, she seemed to have an impulse to express the anger by choking someone. It is my impression that this little girl was imprinted by the trauma and that the trauma started to express itself at a later age in her actual behavior pattern.

There is a body of evidence indicating that it *does* matter how very young children are treated and that their impressions of the people and the world around them are built in at a very young age and will persist tenaciously through the developmental cycle.

Another assumption that parents make is that children cannot read minds. While children cannot literally read minds, the younger the child, the more expert the ability to read cues such as body language and voice tone. Young children are especially perceptive, and it can sometimes seem that the child literally has the capacity to read minds. This is another reason why parents and teachers should think positively and picture the child doing positive acts.

Parents should never lie to a child, because it is impossible to get away with it. When my own son was approximately seven years old I came home from work very angry and upset one day. I walked into the house, and he asked, "What's wrong, Daddy? Are you mad?" I was surprised that he was able to figure this out so quickly, and I asked what he had noticed that gave the impression that I was angry. To my great amazement he was able to tell me that my speed up the driveway with the car was different, my footsteps were heavier, how I opened the door was sharper, and the noise of my briefcase when it hit the floor, as well as my sigh, all tipped him off within seconds. Parents need to understand that hiding major feelings is not possible.

The ninth basic assumption that defeats parents is when they believe that to teach a child something they should try to catch the child doing it wrong. A better strategy is to pay attention to all aspects of the child during the developmental period (to the age of twenty-five) and let the child know that they are really paying attention to what the child is doing "right" most of all. Catching a child doing appropriate acts is extremely reinforcing, while trying to catch a child doing inappropriate things only reinforces the child's wish to be sneaky.

The tenth assumption is that all praise is helpful to children. I believe that this is a real myth. In Dr. Haim Ginott's book titled *Teacher and Child* he states that there are two basic types of praise.[40] Judgmental praise is labeling and saying things like "good boy" or "super kid" or "you're an angel." These labels are hurtful to children and breed dependency and create anxiety.

To build resiliency we want children talking to themselves on the inside with good voices. To do this they have to hear appreciative praise, which describes their action and tells them how others feel about them. It would sound something like this: "I really like the picture that you just drew, and I appreciate the fact that you drew it on top of old newspapers so that you didn't make a big mess." Appreciative praise is the best way to build motivation, and children who think well of themselves are also resilient children.

The next assumption that defeats parents is when parents believe they can raise children without a support system. Parents also have wishes and dreams and want their needs to be gratified, and children are huge time absorbers. There are times when parents absolutely need a break from children in order to pursue their own "narcissistic needs." Most parents can attend to their children 70 percent of the time. The other 30 percent of the time they need to take a break, associate with adults, and get their own needs met. That means in the course of an eight-hour day, which is 480 minutes, 336 minutes are available to really attend to a child. That leaves 144 minutes, or 2½ hours, out of an eight-hour day when it is virtually impossible to be "all there" for the child. Everyone needs respite!

Another reason why parents should not raise children without support systems is because children need to learn multiple coping systems and multiple soothing mechanisms, which means they need different role models to watch. The myth that parents can raise children well without a support system is harmful to children and parents alike.

The last of the dirty dozen assumptions is the belief that in order to correct the child who is being hurtful to another child we must make that child say "sorry." A child who says "sorry" after smacking someone with a Tonka truck generally is not sorry. The reason the child says "sorry" is because the adult is standing there, and the child is smart enough to realize that to get off the hook, or to at least not get punished, he or she needs to comply with what the adult wants.

Adults should insist that the child fix or repair what was done and find something realistic for the child to do to make up. Service takes much more effort and is integrated into the child's system for a much longer period of time.

Children should be made aware of guilt feelings, along with the best way to handle these feelings. Feelings of guilt are taken away when children repair something that they have done. When children make repairs they do not end up provoking others to get themselves punished.

The assumption that children should be let off the hook after they say they are sorry is one of the reasons so many children are not taking responsibility for their own actions. These children are simply looking for ways to get out of personal responsibility, and it is a tragedy when adults and or parents allow this to happen.

Epilogue

Dear Reader,

Thank you for reading this book. I appreciate your perseverance in making it to the end, as I know it was a detailed journey.

Think of this book as a reference library. Read or reread parts of it when you find yourself struggling with similar issues. When children (or your mate) are really getting on your nerves and you feel convinced that they are out to purposely give you a nervous breakdown, reread the sections on projective identification and soothing mechanisms. They may be asking for help on how to manage their own feelings and be looking to you for support.

Always remember that no one should go through life alone, completely without a significant attachment figure. Attachment behaviors and love are a curative elixir for almost any human problem.

It is curious to me how many times a week I see the words *no fear*. It's almost as if we humans are trying to convince ourselves that fear does not exist, at least not in *our* heart. The truth is, everyone is afraid. We fear dying, disease, operations, loneliness, responsibility, hurting someone, being misunderstood, success, failure, maturity, even life itself! We desire things and then find out there is no desire without fear. Fear is everywhere, especially within the human heart. That is why I am so obsessed with attachment. To be truly attached to another person is to be able to share your fear and by sharing it find that it can be endured, even used to live life to the fullest.

For those of you who fear getting your heart broken as you risk loving and attaching, I offer you the words of Scott Peck from his bestselling book *The Road Less Traveled*:

> That internal rending called "the broken heart," which is the especial lot of all sensitive people. Any such person does not live long in this world before the heart is broken. Then as life goes on, the broken heart becomes further sundered into smaller and ever smaller pieces. This is especially the case, of course, with those who deliberately seek union with him whose heart the world insisted upon breaking one more time even after he died...However, they also come to know that, without any question, the important thing is to let the world break the human heart. For one thing, there is room in the broken heart—and only there—for all the sorrows of the world. The broken heart—and only it—is curative, redemptive, of the wasteland around. In addition, it is the very raw material necessary for a strange and important alchemy, which has been described in the words "Your sorrow shall be turned into joy" (John 16:20).[41]

Endnotes

[1] Masud Khan, "The Concept of Cumulative Trauma," *The Psychoanalytic Study of the Child* 18: 286-306.

[2] Beverly James, *Handbook for Treatment of Attachment-Trauma Problems in Children* (New York, NY: The Free Press, 1994), 2.

[3] Bruce D. Perry, Ronnie A. Pollard, Toi L. Blakley, William L. Baker and Domenico Vigilante, "Childhood Trauma: The Neurobiology of Adaptation and Use Dependent Development of the Brain," *Infant Mental Health Journal* 16, no. 4 (winter 1995), www.childtrauma.org/images/stories/Articles/state_trait_95.pdf.

[4] Thomas Lewis, Fari Amini and Richard Lannon, *A General Theory of Love* (New York, NY: Vintage Books, 2001), 88.

[5] Based on the book *The Neverending Story* by Michael Ende (New York, NY: Dutton Children's Books, 1997).

[6] Eric Jensen. *Brain Based Learning: The New Paradigm of Teaching* (Corwin Press, 2008) pg. 68

[7] Margaret Mahler, Fred Pine and Anni Bergman, *The Psychological Birth of the Human Infant: Symbiosis and Individuation* (New York, NY: Basic Books, 1975), pg. 39.

[8] Stanley Greenspan and Nancy Thorndike Greenspan, *First Feelings: Milestones in the Emotional Development of Your Baby and Child* (New York, NY: Viking Press, 1985), 62.

[9] Dorothy Corkille Briggs, *Your Child's Self-Esteem* (New York, NY: Main Street Books, 1988), 65.

[10] G. Sumner and A. Spietz, *NCAST Caregiver/Parent-Child Interaction Teaching Manual* (Seattle: NCAST Publications, 1994).

[11] Donald Winnicott, *Home Is Where We Start From: Essays by a Psychologist* (New York, NY: W.W. Norton & Co., 1990).

[12] Donald Winnicott, *Babies and Their Mothers* (DaCapo Press, Dec. 1992)

[13] Eric Jensen, *Teaching with the Brain in Mind* (Association for Supervision and Curriculum Development, Alexandria, Virginia 1998), pg. 54.

[14] Jane Healy, *Endangered Minds: Why Children Don't Think and What We Can Do About It* (New York, NY: Simon & Schuster, 1999), pg. 45.

[15] Kohut. (American Journal of Psychiatry, January 1987), pg. 3

[16] Briggs, *Your Child's Self-Esteem.*

[17] Haim Ginott, *Teacher and Child* (New York, NY: Macmillan Publishing Company, 1972), pg. 125.

[18] Adele Faber and Elaine Mazlish, *Liberated Parents, Liberated Children: Your Guide to a Happy Family* (New York, NY: Grosset & Dunlap, 1974), 43, pg. 38.

[19] Lenore Terr, *Too Scared to Cry: Psychic Trauma in Childhood* (New York, NY: Basic Books, 1990).

[20] James Prescott, "Early Somato-Sensory Deprivation As an Ortogenetic Process in the Abnormal Development of the Brain and Behavior," *Medical Primatology,* 1970.

[21] John Steinbeck, *East of Eden* (New York, NY: Viking Press, 1952), 270.

[22] Reuven Feuerstein, Rafael S. Feuerstein, Louis H. Falik and Ya'Acov Rand, *The Dynamic Assessment of Cognitive Modifiability* (Jerusalem: The ICELP Press, 2003).

[23] Lewis, Amini and Lannon, *A General Theory,* 88.

[24] Ginott, *Teacher and Child.*

[25] Donald Winnicott, in F. Robert Rodman, *Winnicott: Life and Work* (Cambridge, MA: Da Capo Press, 2003).

[26] Khan, "The Concept of Cumulative Trauma."

[27] Heinz Kohut, *Self Psychology and the Humanities,* ed. C. Strozier (New York, NY: W.W. Norton, 1985).

[28] Ginott, *Teacher and Child.*

[29] Lenore, *Too Scared to Cry.*

[30] James, *Handbook for Treatment,* 1994, pg. 69.

[31] Kahn, "Cumulative Trauma."

[32] Mahler, Pine and Bergman, *Psychological Birth.*

[33] Robert A. Furman and Erna Furman, "Intermittent Decathexis—A Type of Parental Dysfunction," *The International Journal of Psychoanalysis* 65 (1984): 423-433.

[34] Paul Minear, "Eyes of Faith," *Journal of Bible and Religion* 15, no. 1 (1947), 59.

[35] Mary Ainsworth, M. Blehar, E. Walter, S. Wall, "Patterns of Attachment," 1978.

[36] Main, M. & Solomon, J. (1986) "Discovery of a new, insecure-disor-ganized/disoriented attachment pattern. In M. Yogman & T.B. Brancton (Eds.) Affective development in infancy" pp. 95-124. Norwood, NJ: Ablex.

[37] Ruby K. Payne, *A Framework for Understanding Poverty* (Baytown, TX: RFT Publishing Co., 1998), 11.

[38] James Garbarino, *Lost Boys: Why Our Sons Turn Violent and How We Can Help Them* (New York, NY: Simon and Schuster, 2000).

[39] Perry et al., "Childhood Trauma."

[40] Ginott, *Teacher and Child.*

[41] Scott Peck, *The Road Less Traveled* (New York: Simon & Schuster, 2002).

CPSIA information can be obtained at www.ICGtesting.com
Printed in the USA
LVOW10s1219070115

421766LV00012B/284/P